W9-CNE-589

VANISHING FLEECE

VANISHING FLEECE

Adventures in American Wool

CLARA PARKES

ABRAMS PRESS, NEW YORK

Copyright © 2019 Clara Parkes

Jacket © 2019 Abrams

Published in 2019 by Abrams Press, an imprint of ABRAMS. All rights reserved. No portion of this book may be reproduced, stored in a retrieval system, or transmitted in any form or by any means, mechanical, electronic, photocopying, recording, or otherwise, without written permission from the publisher.

Library of Congress Control Number: 2018958831

ISBN: 978–1-4197–3531–8
eISBN: 978–1-68335–682–0

Printed and bound in the United States

10 9 8 7 6 5 4 3 2 1

Abrams books are available at special discounts when purchased in quantity for premiums and promotions as well as fundraising or educational use. Special editions can also be created to specification. For details, contact specialsales@abramsbooks.com or the address below.

Abrams Press® is a registered trademark of Harry N. Abrams, Inc.

ABRAMS The Art of Books
195 Broadway, New York, NY 10007
abramsbooks.com

for Eugene

CONTENTS

INTRODUCTION

GIRL MEETS BALE

RHINEBECK, NEW YORK. A series of debacles had left me at a daylong signing at one of the country's biggest sheep and wool festivals, all doped-up on migraine meds and with my underwear on backward. Let's just say I was not at my best. Late in the afternoon, I noticed a tall, distinguished-looking man standing a few paces away from my table. I assumed he was waiting for one of the people in line, but when the line disappeared he still stood there, studying me with an inscrutable smile. Finally he approached and held out his hand. "My name is Eugene Wyatt," he said. "I raise the largest flock of purebred Saxon Merino sheep in the United States."

My heart skipped a beat. I'd made a life out of traveling the world in search of noteworthy farms, flocks, and people to write about. Here I'd hit the jackpot. Eugene had eyes the color of a Swiss lake, crisp and piercing. He wore a barn jacket that had clearly seen the inside of a barn, with scratches and stains that added to his rugged mystique. He could've easily been Robert Redford's older brother. He had that presence about him.

We immediately got to talking. Talk turned to correspondence, which turned to a friendship of mutual respect that endured for years. When I began investigating making a line of yarn for a national company, Eugene was the first person I asked for fiber. He asked smart, tough questions that made it clear the business move wasn't in my best interest. I canceled the yarn line, but I kept Eugene's wool in the back of my mind. Surely there had to be a way we could work together?

"Also, I wonder where you are concerning the yarn project we spoke about a year or so ago. The reason I'm asking is that I have a 676-pound bale of scoured Saxon Merino wool. Right now it's more than I need . . ."

About a year later, the email came. He filled me in on how shearing and lambing had gone and how his wool had performed at the lab. Every year he sent samples to the Yocom-McColl Wool Testing Lab in Denver for analysis. It's the last independent commercial lab of its kind in the United States, still operated by its founder and now-octogenarian Angus McColl. Using high-tech equipment, Angus's team measures things like average fiber length, strength, curvature, cleanliness, and diameter. That last one is measured in microns, or millionths of a meter. Most "fine" Merino wool falls between 18.6 and 19.5 microns, while human hair averages 75 microns and cashmere ranges from 14 to 19 microns. That year, Eugene's clip was trending between 17.4 and 18.7 microns—on the finest end of Merino and squarely in the range of cashmere. He was pleased.

I'd gotten similar emails from him before, but this time, he added a curious paragraph at the end:

"Also, I wonder where you are concerning the yarn project we spoke about a year or so ago. The reason I'm asking is that I have a 676-pound bale of scoured Saxon Merino wool. Right now it's more than I need . . ."

Eugene always chose his words very carefully. He didn't leave an ellipsis because he'd forgotten what else he wanted to say. He'd left me an invitation. Could I think of any fitting use for that bale? Such an amount of wool, 676 pounds, is tricky. It's not enough to start a yarn company or even, for that matter, a yarn line. But it's way more than any reasonable human being needs for her own personal pleasure. (I'll let you debate what constitutes "reasonable.")

Still, the question remained: What could I do with it?

A crazy idea began to form in my head. An epic, exciting, terrifying idea. Before I could stop it, all the details were there. I knew exactly what I could do with that bale.

The entire project landed in my lap like a fully decorated cake tossed from a moving car. I grabbed it instinctively before my brain had a chance to talk me out of it. But instead of a cake, it was a 676-pound bale of wool. I spent the next ten months trying to persuade myself it was a bad idea, trying to avoid thinking about it, trying to pretend I had a choice in the matter. But in my heart of hearts I'd already committed. My fate was sealed; the bale was a done deal.

As crude oil ships by the barrel and apples by the peck, wool moves about in bales. Measuring the approximate size of a clawfoot bathtub and weighing two-thirds the weight of a grand piano, a bale contains billions of tightly compressed wool fibers held in place with taut steel wires and wrapped with a thick coat of plastic. You can't move one without the aid of a pallet jack, a forklift, or at least three professional weight lifters. A bale is a presence and a commitment.

Most normal people would, upon being offered a chance to purchase an entire bale of wool, likely respond with a polite, if not somewhat confused, "No thank you." Unless you operate your own

---

The entire project landed in my lap like a fully decorated cake tossed from a moving car. I grabbed it instinctively before my brain had a chance to talk me out of it.

As crude oil ships by the barrel and apples by the peck, wool moves about in bales. Measuring the approximate size of a claw-foot bathtub and weighing two-thirds the weight of a grand piano, a bale contains billions of tightly compressed wool fibers held in place with taut steel wires and wrapped with a thick coat of plastic. You can't move one without the aid of a pallet jack, a forklift, or at least three professional weight lifters. A bale is a presence and a commitment.

ready-to-wear clothing line, you probably don't need enough wool to make 170 blankets, or 650 sweaters, or 1,500 pairs of socks. Especially if the wool hasn't even been spun into yarn yet.

But this was no ordinary bale. Eugene had spent more than thirty years tirelessly breeding and culling his flock to refine the bloodline of this rare, prized strain of Merino sheep whose wool is as fine as cashmere. That single bale represented a year's worth of work for my farmer friend. He could have easily sold it for twice what he was quoting me. Or he could've used it to make more of his own yarn that he sold at New York's Union Square Greenmarket every Saturday. But for reasons unknown to me at the time, Eugene wanted me—a person who only writes about yarn and has no manufacturing experience whatsoever—to have it.

Since 2000, I'd had a successful career as the world's first and probably only professional yarn critic. I got to teach and write articles, to be on the radio and TV, and to write books. By the time Eugene's bale came into my life, I'd been doing the same thing, chewing the same cud, for thirteen years. Maybe Eugene saw it first, but I soon realized it myself: My interest was starting to wane. Everything began to look the same; every story seemed to be repetitive. I was having a harder and harder time summoning enthusiasm for my subject. I felt like I was on the verge of coasting, just slicing and dicing the same bit of knowledge in as many permutations as possible to make it interesting to me again, as well as to my readers. Turn passion into a profession and the spark inevitably fades, I figured. I plodded on.

It didn't help that nine-tenths of the world already thought my job was a joke. Knitting is laden with so many cultural stereotypes that the notion of someone making a full-time career out of reviewing yarn made most people laugh and say, "No, seriously, what do you do?" When I'd say I'd been doing it for more than a decade, they usually backed away.

But as soon as the bale appeared, I had a vision for something completely different—and it filled me with excitement and fear. Since the whole thing felt as outlandishly epic as Ahab's quest for the great white whale in *Moby-Dick*, I began calling this my "great white bale." Only I was Ishmael, the book's narrator who'd never been on a whaling ship before. I'd sailed the seven seas of yarn, but never as a manufacturer.

I would buy that bale and use it to walk through the steps that commercial yarn companies take every time they make yarn in the United States. Not just any yarn, but good yarn—and I would do this not as a critic, but as a customer. How better to appreciate other people's work than by walking in their shoes?

After some calculations based on very little actual fact, I figured I could divvy up the bale into four batches. Each batch would go to a different kind of mill, with its own processing technique and equipment. I could even bring color into the equation and try out the fibers on different types of dyes and dyers. I'd been wanting to go back to school, and here it was, an accelerated master's degree program in yarn making. I'd give it a year.

My curriculum would follow the life cycle of wool yarn, from shearing and scouring to spinning and dyeing. I'd find the weak spots, the places where things tend to go wrong—and I'd learn how to avoid them. And perhaps, just perhaps, I'd have more understanding and appreciation for the people who are trying to do this for a living.

I looked into whether I could expand the curriculum higher in the food chain and manufacture actual goods with my wool. But I quickly learned that what seemed daunting to me (my 676 pounds of wool) wasn't nearly enough fiber for any manufacturing endeavor beyond, say, hand-crocheted amigurumi kitten key chains. And it certainly wouldn't be enough to launch my own ready-to-wear line. (Which is good because I never know what to wear anyway.) I'd take it as far as yarn and let others make of it what they may.

Even at the price Eugene quoted me, this yarn degree would not come cheap. Lacking a conventional student loan option for my self-made master's degree, I had another idea: What if I opened up this project to other people, for both the risks and the rewards? What if I sold them a seat on my bus? Adventures are far more fun in the company of good people, and these would be my people. I'd share every step of the process in words and photos and videos in a password-protected bunker online called, fittingly, the Great White Bale.

I gave people two "seating" options on this adventure. The Armchair Travelers got the most affordable seats with great big windows so they could follow along online. A smaller group of Explorers paid more and received souvenirs, by which I mean the skeins of yarn from each mill adventure. This option added a sort of scratch-and-sniff component to the program, and it kept me from ending up with more yarn than I could ever use in my lifetime. By the end of the year, we'd all emerge with newly minted Master's of Yarn-Making degrees. It was crowdfunded education at its very best.

Curiosity about the American textiles industry was on the rise, and small-batch, breed-specific yarns-with-stories were gaining greater acceptance.

I suspect part of me knew I needed other people to keep me accountable, lest I chicken out at the very first phone call and end up with an unused bale of wool in my barn—right next to the boxes of knitting-themed notecards I used to sell, the exercise bike I used to ride, and the sign from my store (Clara's Window) that I ran for three years and that, in actual fact, had two windows. I am nothing if not full of ideas. It's the maintenance that trips me up. But perhaps if I knew a thousand people were watching my every move, it wouldn't.

My timing was good. Curiosity about the American textiles industry was on the rise, and small-batch, breed-specific yarns-with-stories were gaining greater acceptance. Knitters were starting to sniff out yarns from smaller sources, even if they cost more—and consumers, too, were gladly adding a few bucks to the bill for a pair of wool socks entirely grown in this country. After so many years of fetishizing farmers' markets and free-range everything, the general public was finally catching on that what we put on our bodies is just as important as what we put in them.

Within a matter of hours of announcing it, all of the Explorer spots in my Great White Bale project were taken and hundreds of Armchair Travelers had signed up. Like that, the project was funded. I was stunned. It seemed that many people were eager to follow along and learn something new. They trusted me not to disappear with their money halfway through the project, as a few others had already done in the knitting world. Or maybe they were betting on a ringside seat to a catastrophic failure that would force me to fake my own death on social media just to escape the

*More than just admiring the machinery
and fondling the finished product, I met
the people doing this work. And that
turned out to be the most important aspect
of the whole experience.*

pitchforks? I'll never be sure. All I knew was that this crazy thing
was really happening.

Everything about this was miles beyond my comfort zone, and
I liked the degree of fear it sparked in me. I'd never actually seen a
bale of wool up close, much less approached a commercial mill about
making yarn. I didn't even know how I'd get the bale shipped to me,
or where I'd store it. (My long-suffering partner, Clare, had already
declared the barn off-limits.) I just knew that if I didn't give this a try,
if I didn't scratch this itch, I was on the fast track to becoming that
bored restaurant critic who can't even boil an egg at home.

Over the next twelve months, the journey would take me on
thirty-four takeoffs and landings and along 1,590 miles driven in
eight rental cars. I traveled from Maine to California, Texas, New
York, Massachusetts, Pennsylvania, Wisconsin, and Virginia. The
actual order of events didn't always follow a straight line, so, for the
sake of clarity, I've adjusted the chronology here to match the natural
life cycle of wool fibers. We go from shearing on the farm to washing at a steamy scouring plant, from opening the bale to shipping
batches of wool to four different mills that had agreed to take on
what I didn't realize until later was an absurdly demanding proposi-
tion. Color entered the picture too, with explorations in natural dye,
hand-dyeing with acid dyes, and large-scale commercial dyeing.

More than just admiring the machinery and fondling the finished product, I met the people doing this work. And that turned
out to be the most important aspect of the whole experience. Their

stories ran the gamut from heartbreaking to life-affirming, and they painted an overarching picture of an industry and way of life that have been hard-hit but refuse to die. I witnessed, on a profound level, what's at stake and how much all of this matters.

At a time when other industries seem eager to build walls around their work to keep prying eyes out, I encountered nothing but generosity and kindness. People were hungry to tell me about their work, to explain things as many times as it took, and to help me along on my way. I learned the power of asking for help—and accepting it—and I emerged with a keen appreciation not just for the work, but for the people still doing it.

What follows isn't a manual on how to make yarn, although you'll certainly get some pointers. I like to think of it as a portrait of an extraordinary slice of American life. It's a tribute to the skill, energy, sacrifice, and optimism of the few people who are still moving forward a domestic industry that globalization has done its best to destroy. And it's the story of what can happen when you take a risk and try something new.

The story belongs as much to America's sheep ranchers and shearers and textile workers as it does me. May it inspire you to think about wool a little differently, and to step outside of your own comfort zone and catch a few cakes yourself.

CHAPTER 1
WOOL HARVEST

CHECK EUGENE WYATT'S CALENDAR on any given year and you'll find a giant X on the first Monday in March. That's when a crew arrives to this sheep farm in New York State for the annual rite of shearing. Depending on the year, Eugene will have upward of five hundred sheep to be shorn. The whole process takes as long as three days to complete. Eugene times everything else in his year around this date, and it's one that cannot be missed. Just a few weeks later, the ewes will begin delivering their lambs, and all coats must be off before that happens.

I'm here to touch raw Saxon Merino wool on the hoof and meet the sheep and people behind it. This is my Michael Pollan moment, but instead of partaking in, say, the slaughter of a pig, I'm visiting the farm where the wool in my bale came from, watching the sheep get shorn, and better getting to know Eugene, the remarkable shepherd of this equally remarkable flock.

Sheep didn't always need our help removing their coats. They used to shed each spring, leaving tufts of wool snagged on bushes and fence posts and in the grabby hands of the humans tending them (the latter being a process called "rooing"). For more than ten thousand years, sheep offered a one-stop haberdashery for all our needs. Lacking the distraction of cell phones or social media, we had plenty of time to separate out each kind of fiber by hand for its optimal application. Short tender fibers went in the next-to-skin pile while long pointy ones went in the durable goods basket, not to mention all the various shades of brown, tan, gray, and black that were further sorted for colorwork.

Modern sheep breeds have coats that are bright, fine, and uniform, and they come off only when we say so.

All that came to a halt at the onset of the Industrial Revolution, which conveniently coincided with the rise of selective breeding as a scientific practice. You'd think we would've caught on sooner, but it wasn't until the mid-1700s, boosted by a British agriculturalist named Robert Bakewell, that we realized we could change what was born by simply choosing which animals were allowed to breed. Random tendencies, if carefully bred from generation to generation, could eventually become the norm. We were rolling up our sleeves and playing Darwin (who was inspired by Bakewell), but it wasn't always the fittest that ended up surviving. Often, it was the most desirable.

By the late 1700s, we no longer valued different textures and colors as much. We wanted one thing: brilliant, fine, white wool. We also wanted to be in control of when the wool came off the sheep. For the most part we succeeded. Modern sheep breeds have coats that are bright, fine, and uniform, and they come off only when we say so. Which, in Eugene's case, is always that first Monday in March.

Eugene's farm is in Goshen, New York, a sleepy hamlet some sixty miles north of Manhattan. Settled in 1714, it now boasts one chain hotel, seven pizza restaurants, a diner, and a town square that's actually a triangle. Its architectural claim to fame is the Orange County Government Center, a crazy, boxy, iconically Brutalist jumble of glass and concrete that was somehow permitted to be built in 1967 and that the locals have been trying to demolish ever since. They finally reached a compromise. By the time you read this, some of the much-contested structure will have been relegated to the history books.

Eugene rents 140 acres with several outbuildings from a farmer south of town. He pays rent on part of the property, and the farmer grows hay on the rest—which Eugene then buys back for his flock in eight-hundred-pound bales, fourteen per week, at $38 apiece. It's a complicated form of extra rent he finds both convenient and ironic, since the hay fields are fertilized by his sheep.

I'd driven down the night before and was lingering over breakfast and a dull mug of coffee at the Goshen Plaza Diner when the insecurities began to hit. Visiting Eugene on his home turf had seemed like a great idea. But as I drove the quiet country roads out of town, my crisis of confidence deepened. I'd built up quite the illusions about him and his flock by then, and I felt so sure my image was right, I'd bet my reputation on it. What if I was wrong? What if I'd misread him completely and his place was a disaster, the animals were living in filth, and he had naked-lady mudflaps on his truck? I could coach myself through that worry well enough. But what if my questions came off as naive and he regretted ever offering me his fibers? My god, what if he was the one who'd built up grand expectations about me that I couldn't possibly fulfill? My Michael Pollan moment was missing just one thing: the confidence and bravery of an actual Michael Pollan.

A winding, narrow road and deep ditches on either side brought my attention back to the present. The trees were still bare. Rolling farmland was dotted with rumpled old barns surrounded by emerald green grass and occasional exposed earth the color of brownie batter. Every few miles I saw fresh, boxy McMansions creeping over the horizon like redcoats on the advance. Eugene had told me he was still in Goshen only because a development referendum had stopped his landlord from subdividing, "for now."

Following Eugene's instructions, I pulled into a farm at the top of a hill and parked next to another car. There were no sheep in sight. Not until I was about ten yards from a low cinder-block building with vines climbing through its cracked casement windows did

I begin to hear signs of life. A person's voice, then the humming of electric shears, the quiet bleat of a sheep, a woman's voice singing. Dolly Parton.

As my eyes adjusted to the darkness inside, Eugene spotted me and came over.

"I'm ready for my close-up!" he said in an exaggerated southern falsetto.

He'd worn his best overalls just for my visit, he said. His hands were bare, and on his head was a faded purple knitted hat. So far so good.

An iPod was connected to portable speakers balanced on a low wall. A faded floral tablecloth covered a shelf under a nearby window. On it, a vase of tulips glowed in a ray of sunlight, while old china plates held cookies, brownies, and raspberry bars.

"You're just in time," Eugene said, and began walking me through what was happening.

They were borrowing the landlord's dairy barn for shearing, he explained. Its space was better equipped to facilitate what needed to happen over the next few days. Eugene's barn and pasture were just over the next hill. "We'll go there in a while," he said.

To our far right, three shearers stood on makeshift plywood boards, their bodies bent over sheep splayed in awkward but effective positions. Their hands moved quickly and confidently, the metal blades working like snowplows to push thick white strips of fiber off the sheep's bodies.

Shorn fleeces were being gathered off the plywood floor and carried to a large slatted metal "skirting" table—a giant lazy Susan of sorts—where they were flung like pizza dough into the air, landing fully open on the table, their sheep-shaped outline still intact.

Three helpers immediately swooped in and began plucking dirty and undesirable bits from around the edges of the fleece, tossing them on the bare ground under the table. I could see no rhyme or reason to their work. Masses of grass and hay were being left, dark ugly bits around the edges stayed, too, while other areas were immediately—and with great intention—pulled and tossed.

"Would you like to have a turn?" Eugene asked, and they all stepped aside to make room for me. Overwhelmed by a feeling of total ineptitude, I pulled out my camera and urged them to keep working so I could document what they were doing. I'd never properly skirted a fleece before, but they were looking at me as if I were the expert.

As crucial as shearing is (and it *is* critical to a sheep's health), skirting and classing are even more critical if you hope to get good money for your wool. Skirting is the process of removing inferior and contaminated fibers that would lower the value of your wool. Classing takes things one step further, grouping "like" wools with "like" wools so that that you can sell the finest wool in your clip for a better price. A good classer can gauge a fleece's fineness by sight and touch to within a micron. A bad classer can really mess things up.

Eugene wasn't selling his wool to someone else, so receiving top dollar for his clip wasn't really a concern. His flock had so little variability in fineness that all the fleeces from his Saxon Merinos were being bundled together—so they didn't need an experienced classer on hand either.

But they were still skirting. Eugene explained that the wool on the belly, the head (or "top knot"), and the legs ("britches") had already been left behind on the shearing board. "They're dirty," he said. "Not uniform."

Any kind of contamination—be it excess vegetable matter or urine-stained locks or even strands of polypropylene from a stray gate tie—will cause a yarn to spin poorly and lower the overall yield of that year's wool clip. "Yield" was another big thing for Eugene. Yield represents the amount of clean wool left after the raw wool has been scoured and all the dirt and grease removed. The higher the yield, the more usable wool you get from each sheep, the more potentially profitable your operation. American Delaine Merino sheep (the most common breed of Merino in the United States) tend to grow greasier wool, bringing their yield down to an average of 50 percent, sometimes less. Eugene's flock regularly yielded 65 percent, occasionally higher. This was another indication that his attempts to breed to true Saxon Merino standards were paying off.

Back at the skirting table, shorter nubbins fell like confetti through the open slats and onto the ground below, where they'd later be raked up and used for garden compost. Those were second cuts, from areas where the shearer had run over the same spot twice. You remove those for much the same reason you check your pockets for Kleenex before doing laundry: They'll clump together during processing and leave behind little tufts of fluff in your yarn, ultimately making the fabric pill more quickly.

Tidied fleeces were then gathered and stuffed into a tall, clear plastic bag—"I get them from Mid-States Wool," Eugene said, "four bucks apiece"—until even the tallest person standing on an upturned milk crate couldn't fit any more inside. It took two people to wrestle the bag to a far wall, where several others already stood, full from a busy morning.

While five hundred sheep seemed huge to me, it was tiny compared with the bigger sheep operators out west, whose flocks number in the thousands and, in a few cases, the tens of thousands. I say "operators," but they're really family-run ranches where the sheep are given abundant range to run. Where wool is concerned, there is no such thing as factory farming.

At shearing time, those bigger folks use hydraulic presses to jam their wool into five-hundred-pound square packs, Eugene explained. The square ones fit better in overseas shipping containers. But smaller farm flocks like his use these "sausage" packs or ones made from burlap. They hold a more manageable one to two hundred pounds of fleece, but their awkward shape makes them harder to transport in efficient loads.

Later that week Eugene would rent a twenty-four-foot truck and drive the unwieldy bags of wool to the defunct Bollman Hat Company scouring plant in Adamstown, Pennsylvania, where they would join other bags from other farms on a bigger truck to Bollman's new facility in Texas. There, his fibers would be scoured, baled up, and shipped to the Green Mountain Spinnery in Vermont, where they'd be spun into yarn before being returned to the farm, the cycle complete.

I glanced to my left and did a double take: Hundreds of curious eyes stared back at me. The sheep had been brought into the barn the day before and were standing in clusters, patiently waiting their turn. They hadn't had food or water for a day, but nobody appeared to be complaining. "It just makes them a little more willing to cooperate," Eugene explained. "It also empties them out so they don't shit on the shearing floor."

A makeshift metal wire fence kept them from having the run of the barn, while another line of fence blocked off the back door, preventing them from escaping. These were the ewes, Eugene explained—a whole barn full of pregnant ladies who'd be delivering their lambs in just a few weeks. They were the easiest. The feisty rams came last.

In North America, most sheep are shorn in spring, ideally three to four weeks before the ewes start to lamb. You shear before lambing for much the same reason you'd mow turf before a golf tournament—to make it easier for lambs to find the teat and, with it, the vital antibodies from the ewe's colostrum that builds their own immune system. You're also eliminating any chance of those lambs accidentally nursing on manure-laden wool, which they can do, and which can kill them.

As with humans, the hormonal surge ewes experience at lambing produces a weak spot in their fleece. By timing shearing so that this weak spot occurs near the outer edge of the fiber and not smack-dab in the center, a shepherd can produce stronger, i.e., more valuable, wool. When the weak spot falls in the middle, those fibers will likely break in half during processing, leading to shorter fibers in a fabric that will pill more quickly. Shearing now will also keep sheep more comfortable during the hot summer months, while giving Eugene plenty of time to vaccinate the pregnant ewes so that they'll be able to provide those antibodies to their lambs.

Despite the speed and simplicity of this annual ritual, some continue to publicly question whether shearing is harmful to sheep. Some of those people (I'm looking at you, PETA) have gone so far as to urge us not to wear wool at all—the argument being that sheep need their coats more than we do, and that petrochemical-based fibers are somehow kinder. In actual fact, all wool-growing sheep need to be shorn at least once a year. Since their genetic trait to shed has been lost over thousands of years of cohabitation with us, it falls upon us, their responsible human companions, to remove their fleece for them. If we don't, their health and hygiene are quickly imperiled.

The longer a sheep goes unshorn, the greater its risk of "casting," or losing its balance and tipping onto its back. Unlike beetles, sheep lack the ability to right themselves once this happens. Eventually the gases in the sheep's rumen build up and press against the diaphragm, causing the sheep to slowly suffocate.

Worse yet is the increased risk of flystrike. (You might want to skip ahead if you're squeamish.) In sheep, the built-up urine and feces around the back area, or "breech," can be particularly attractive to parasitic flies. The flies lay eggs on the soiled wool, and when the maggots hatch, they bury themselves deep into the dark, warm folds of the sheep's skin and start feasting on flesh. While sheep with more wrinkles in their skin can be particularly vulnerable, all sheep are at risk—especially if they are not shorn annually.

In Australia, where acute flystrike is particularly common, a prevention technique was developed in the 1930s by a shearer named John Mules. Called "mulesing," the procedure involves surgically removing excess skin around a lamb's breech. While this "butt-lift" helps prevent flystrike, it is usually performed without anesthetics, which has raised concerns among animal-rights groups.

Today mulesing is practiced only in Australia and only by some producers. Others have successfully implemented humane prevention techniques and can offer non-mulesed Australian wool. Still, the bad press on mulesing led many to conclude that any purchase of wool, no matter where it's from or how the sheep were raised, is a vote for cruelty. If you could see what was happening in Goshen, you'd know this is simply not true.

All of the Saxon Merino sheep in Eugene's flock are direct descendants of five prize-winning Saxon Merino studs he flew to the United States from Australia in 1990, just a few years after Australia lifted its ban on their exportation. Their bloodlines had reached Australia from what is now Germany, where they'd been a gift to Prince Xavier the Elector of Saxony from his cousin Charles III of Spain. If Merino is to wool what gold is to precious metals, Saxon Merino is among the purest and most highly valued variants.

At shearing time, weather is always the biggest concern. A freak ice storm the day after shearing can be devastating to the flock, just as snow or rain can be to the wool during the days before. You don't want to remove a sheep's insulation right before an extreme weather event; nor do you want to shear a wet sheep, as the wool will rot very quickly once it's bagged.

If Merino is to wool what gold is to precious metals, Saxon Merino is among the purest and most highly valued variants.

Fortunately, the weather was in our favor: dry and cold the whole week. The high was in the mid-thirties. The sun was warm and bright, although it was much, much colder in the shade. I'd been warned to wear warm clothes. Unsure how dirty the whole shearing experience would be at his farm, I'd bought a cheap puffy purple jacket that looked ridiculous and made me feel instantly out of place. We kept going back into Eugene's truck to talk. It had no naked-lady mudflaps, though it *did* have leopard-print seat covers—but they were covered with sheepskins and coffee stains.

"My hands can't handle the cold too much," he admitted. "But I'm eating *this* cookie"—he waved it at me—"so I can take an Aleve for my knees."

Back in the barn, cluster by cluster, the ewes were being moved into increasingly smaller pens, each separated by more flexible metal fencing. By the time they reached the shearing area, they were squished together and easy to maneuver. Flock animals by nature, sheep actually feel safer in such close proximity. They made very little noise at all.

Two of the youngest helpers had been tasked with directing each one-hundred-pound expectant ewe from the pen to the shearer. A tall, skinny boy had been recruited from a neighboring farm, ostensibly for his strength, but the most skilled sheep catcher was Rebecca, a college-bound woman who happened to be an ace hockey player. Her mother, Kris, was working the skirting table, too. She told me she was there purely for the pleasure of touching wool and being around the animals. Later, Eugene told me Kris never takes money from him, although on rare occasions she will accept a skein of yarn or two as payment.

One by one, the sheep were moved to the next available shearer, who stood in special moccasins on the makeshift plywood floor, electric shears in hand. (They need to be aware of the position of their feet at all times, and the moccasins help them do just that.)

*Leave a trail of bloodied flesh and your
days as a shearer will be numbered. In the
wool world, reputation is everything.*

The act of shearing itself takes just a few minutes from start to finish. A champion shearer can do it in a little over two minutes. Most shearing crews are paid per head, giving the larger operations more motivation to go fast. Here, with a finite number of sheep, smaller crew, and set schedule, they were able to be gentler with the animals and steadier with their cuts. It's a tricky balance. You want to get off as much wool as possible, cutting close to the skin without any nicks on the first try. But you also want to leave a fine layer of wool to keep the sheep warm while more grows back. Return for a second cut and you add short, useless fluff to the fleece. Leave a trail of bloodied flesh and your days as a shearer will be numbered. In the wool world, reputation is everything.

Proper shearing involves a series of set positions for the shearer and the sheep, with stances and swooping maneuvers all designed to get maximum fiber off with minimal effort or stress (to the shearer or the animal). Part of this involves plunking the sheep on its butt, like a cat upright on its haunches, legs splayed. In the right hands, a sheep soon enters a trancelike state of submission. You almost have to wake it up when you're done. I felt myself going into a trance just watching.

Released, the sheep usually gives a shake, trots toward the open door, then stops, turns around, and studies where she just was. I watched a few scamper in the other direction, past the skirting table and back toward the waiting sheep—as if to check on them, or warn them, or perhaps just reassure them that it wasn't so bad. Occasionally they had to be retrieved; other times they wandered back on their own. Outside, fresh bales of hay awaited. The ewes clustered around them, chewing, chatting, maybe comparing notes.

This year there had been a changing of the guard among the crew. The man who'd shorn Eugene's flock for years had finally retired, leaving his young assistant, Aaron, in charge. Aaron hails from Western Massachusetts. He grew up around sheep, his older sisters having raised them for 4-H projects. He learned to shear early on, and it took. His hands were gentle and confident, like those of a parent washing a baby.

Aaron brought two new shearers, both of whom compete in national competitions, and both of whom happen to be women. Some of the old-school farmers are still cynical about the presence of women on the shearing floor. Not Eugene. "The fact that they're his shearing partners is good enough for me," he said. Some even say women are better suited to shearing. They certainly are entering the profession in droves now, which can't be a bad thing.

One of the shearers, Emily, brought her young daughter, who spent the day singing songs to the ewes and swinging on anything she could find. She'd accompanied her mom to shearings since she was a baby, so this was home to her. When the skirting table was not in use, she put her teddy bear on it and spun it around and around. Change was afoot at the skirting table, too. A helper they'd seen as a man last year returned, this year, as a radiant woman. All taken in stride.

When we weren't warming up in the truck, Eugene stood in the background, hands in pockets, observing. He wasn't one for idle chatter. Occasionally he'd grab a broom and sweep the board around a shearer who'd just released a sheep. Other times, he'd dip his fingers into a freshly shorn fleece on the skirting table, like a chef checking the work of one of his line cooks. Or he'd sneak off to puff on his pipe. Then I'd find him back on the shearing floor, lying awkwardly on his side, snapping artful pictures with his iPhone. He was nearing seventy, and his Twitter game was sterling.

It seemed surreal. I'd been led to believe that shearing was prime season for man-against-beast testosterone, for nicks and blood, machismo and cursing. I'd been dreading this part of my schooling, being around animals who were traumatized and men who were thriving on traumatizing them. I saw none of that. Instead, the mood was calm, quiet, and orderly, with the same amount of respect for both the people and the sheep. In fact, I might've been the most nervous one there.

I began to suspect that the shearing was just slyly orchestrated propaganda for the purpose of making me go home and start a flock of my own. I'd have to check the back of my car to make sure they hadn't tucked a ewe or two in there. How much of this vibe was pure luck, I wondered, and how much was a direct reflection of Eugene?

I finally mentioned this to one of the women at the shearing table. "Oh, he's much nicer with you here to distract him," she whispered. "It's making everything go so much more smoothly."

I wasn't sure I could claim all the credit, though. This was a year for firsts. Not only was it the first time they'd had women shearers, but it was also the first time they'd ever had music playing, or had a young child hanging around, or been visited by an interviewer with a camera. Whatever the combination, it worked.

Tending a flock of more than five hundred sheep is an ironic pursuit for a man who'd never wanted to have children. "I don't have a job," he liked to say. "I have responsibilities."

Though a bachelor now, Eugene had been married once. He wed his college sweetheart, Bettina. They lived in New York City; she was

---

I began to suspect that the shearing was just slyly orchestrated propaganda for the purpose of making me go home and start a flock of my own.

a successful fashion designer in the Garment District. In 1988, they did what a lot of people in their circles were doing: They bought a forty-acre farm in Sullivan County. It was gorgeous, but something was missing. Attracted by the notion of big beasts with impressive horns, Eugene suggested they raise cattle. Bettina talked him into Merino sheep. Cows scared her, whereas she could use the Merino wool in her garments.

Off they flew to a big livestock show in Louisville. "I didn't even know what a sheep looked like," Eugene said. "But I saw that it had horns, so I said let's get them!"

They connected with an American Delaine Merino breeder in Nevada, loaded five pregnant ewes into the back of a truck, drove them home, and, in Eugene's words, "we sat on them, like Easter eggs, until they hatched." The plan was to let the ewes and their offspring mow the lawn and keep the weeds under control. But the minute the lambs arrived, Eugene was hooked.

Two years later, he flew to Australia, toured several top sheep stations with an agent, and bid on five prize-winning Saxon Merino stud rams. He won the bid, flew the rams back to the United States, and began his Saxon Merino flock in earnest.

Eugene is the first to admit that he knew absolutely nothing. "Every time a sheep coughed," he said, "we called the vet." But he was humble enough to know how little he knew, to hire those who did know more, and to learn from them. "Employees are your teachers," he said. He also read everything he could find.

When Eugene first showed his sheep at the American Delaine Merino Association show, he took home a trophy but with a warning about size. Standards in the United States are skewed, as is everything else, toward bigger being better. "We breed for big," he said. "It's the culture of the carny. They've got Ferris wheels right outside the show ring."

Instead of embracing those standards and bulking up his flock, Eugene pulled out of the association. He stuck to his principles, breeding to true Australian Saxon Merino standards, which still reward small and fine.

In the world of sheep, there is a generally acknowledged correlation between animal size and fiber fineness. The larger the animal's overall frame, the larger the diameter of fiber it grows (and the larger the diameter, the more you'll feel it against your skin). The smaller the frame, the smaller the fiber diameter.

While a larger frame means more meat, which equals greater revenue per animal, Eugene was not willing to compromise on fiber quality—despite the fact that meat represented more than 80 percent of his weekly farm revenue. He told me he doesn't want millions ("Well, who doesn't want millions?"); he'd just like to be able to keep doing this and find a broader market for his yarn. "I don't have much Social Security," he said, "but I'm content."

After an amicable divorce, Eugene moved his flock a few times before finally settling in Goshen, where he now rents a stylish bachelor pad in a converted barn not too far away.

If I've given you the impression that Eugene works alone, let me correct that right now. He has Dominique Herman, the yin to his yang, the nurturing female to his stern, father-like figure. Perhaps a decade or two younger than Eugene, Dominique is short and wiry, with strong hands and intense eyes. The trusting ewes follow her everywhere, lovestruck and hopeful for treats.

I didn't dare ask if they were more than co-shepherds, and it didn't really matter. Theirs was a partnership in the purest sense. Dominique is an insomniac, and the sheep fill those early dark hours, especially in winter. By 4 a.m. she's on the farm to check on them. Later in the day, as she's suppressing yawns, Eugene arrives to see the sheep through to dusk, making sure they're returned to the safer, more protected parts of the farm. Predators are a constant worry.

Dominique helps oversee lambing, stepping in to assist when necessary. She's been known to bring home the occasional

> *"I realized early on," he said, "that this was either a really expensive hobby or a poorly paying business. You have to be clever."*

semi-frozen lamb and nurse it back to health, cutting up old sweater sleeves to keep the tiny creature warm until it can take care of itself.

When several of the sheep contracted a deer-born virus that causes paralysis, Dominique didn't give up. She researched the virus and came up with a sling-like contraption that allowed the affected sheep to stand outside, assisted, in the sun. Her voice wavered when she told me how, just that morning, one sheep stood up on her own. "She still has a weird little limp." She pointed her out from the group. "But can you believe it? She's walking. It's a miracle."

While Dominique nurtures and nurses, Eugene has the ultimate authority: He decides which lambs will live and which will die. At least that's the illusion he wants to give. In fact, he's been swayed on multiple occasions to spare at least one or two of Dominique's favorites. But when it's time to see the unfortunates onto that truck, it's Eugene who leads them on, puts the keys in the ignition, and drives away.

"I drop them off at the slaughterhouse," he said, "where these ghoulish men thank me and wish me a nice day. An hour later, the animals have been dispatched, and they come back to the farm in a box in the back of my truck." Death is an essential part of any large-scale, financially viable sheep farm, though I sensed that it was a hard reality even for Eugene.

"I realized early on," he said, "that this was either a really expensive hobby or a poorly paying business. You have to be clever."

For Eugene, that cleverness is rooted in offering the highest-end products—the gold standard of wool yarn, gourmet sausages, and plump garlic cloves grown in fields that have been fertilized by his flock—at one of the finest farmers' markets in the country. Every week at the Union Square Greenmarket in New York City, people pay a premium for the very best.

Just as the quality of a garden reflects the quality of the seeds planted, the quality of Eugene's flock begins with its rams. While the ladies were getting coiffed uphill, these prized royal beasts had been sequestered in a pasture by the main barn, the road to which was deeply rutted by the recent spring thaw.

We drove down to see them in Eugene's truck. A small cluster of rams lazed about, their heads crowned with majestic swirls of horns. They were surprisingly docile. A few got up and sauntered over to greet me and see if I had a snack. Others stayed put, eyes closed, blissed out by the warmth of the sun.

One ram sat alone in a separate fenced-in area. "That's our Dishley Merino," Eugene explained. He was kept separate because the other rams beat up on him. Dishley Merino is the early name for a breed now known as Île-de-France—which explains how this guy got the nickname "the Frenchman." Dominique insisted he was a love, Ferdinand the Bull in ovine form. She'd convinced Eugene to keep him, although Eugene still insisted he'd like to drive over him with his truck.

The nearby outdoor dye studio was a cluster of propane burners and metal pots on a concrete slab by the barn. They dye all the yarn that goes to the market, often experimenting with natural dyeing. "We're in the process of training a new hand-dyer," Eugene said, standing back to study orange and turquoise skeins swaying in the breeze.

"Those are too garish," he said.

His art-critic demeanor hinted at Eugene's other past. After ditching chemistry and pre-med at UC Berkeley in the 1960s, he landed a series of jobs at art galleries in San Francisco. He had no idea what he was doing at first, so he went to all the museums and galleries he could find. He read, and he studied. Eventually he worked his way up to managing a gallery on Geary Boulevard. When that business partnership went south, he followed a goldsmith's advice and moved to Paris. Again, he had no idea what he was doing—"I didn't even know how to say 'fuck' in French"—but after four years of bouncing from girlfriend to girlfriend, he was fluent. "Whenever I had nothing to do," he said, "I went to the museum."

Which is exactly what he does most Saturdays after finishing up at the Greenmarket. Eugene's blog is just as likely to have an analysis of a show at the Met, or of a single painting or poem or film, as it is to include mention of the farm or the sheep. He's especially passionate about Proust.

As we walked toward the barn, a small cat darted by. Another perched on a stone. We passed through an old door whose screen was kicked open at foot level. I saw more cats. One was in the windowsill; another peeked out from a box on a shelf. A black-and-white one peered at us through a doorway, his head tilted in a way I thought signaled inquisitiveness.

"That's our five-hundred-dollar cat," Eugene said, referring to the cat's remarkably high vet bills. "We call him Sideways because his head has always been crooked like that."

Neighbors have gotten wise to the presence of cat lovers on the farm and are always dropping off stray cats and kittens. Dominique may be soft on the sheep, but that's nothing compared to Eugene's devotion to these cats. Those who get along live a good life here. They keep the place free of rats and mice. The broken screen door allows them freedom of movement that, in turn, keeps them from using the inside of the barn as their litterbox.

In another room, a long row of empty coolers stood at attention, freshly washed and waiting for the next market day. In a dark back room, sheep skins were heaped with salt to cure. The smell was faintly unsettling, or maybe it was just the sight of the skins that did it. This barn was where the sheep ultimately came to rest.

As already mentioned, the bulk of Eugene's farm revenue doesn't come from wool. It comes from the lamb and sausages. Until a few years ago, the sausages were all made by a man in Pennsylvania. But his operation was shut down by the USDA soon after he turned eighty-two, presumably because he could or would not conform to new regulations. Dominique suggested Robert ("Bobby") Matuszewski, a Culinary Institute of America–trained chef nearby who'd been gaining acclaim for his smoked meats and sausages.

"How far away is he?" I asked.

"He's just over . . . well . . . let's go there," Eugene said. "Want to?"

Into his truck we piled again, and soon we were careening over ruts and potholes that explained all the coffee stains in his truck. A tiny plastic lamb was jammed in the dashboard air vents ("I can't resist picking one up every time I go to the feed store," Dominique told me earlier). Eugene is a slow, ponderous driver, the kind who takes so long to look both ways before turning that a car inevitably appears out of the first place he looked, forcing him to jam on the brakes. Which had already happened to us twice. He also doesn't seem inclined to wear his seat belt.

After all this time, Eugene has become deeply attuned to his flock's nuances and needs. "You have to be," he said. "Sheep won't tell you if they're sick." He has developed a keen instinct for all animal behavior, including that of other people. I felt that when we first met at the New York Sheep and Wool Festival. He'd studied me for quite a while at a polite distance before coming up and introducing himself. Only years later did he offer me his wool.

He must've known I would eventually say yes, and that I was the right person for his fibers. While I spent months dithering about the decision, he patiently watched and waited and never pushed. When I finally agreed, he wrote back, "I like working with you at the speed you work, when you're ready." It was the first time anyone had praised the often ponderous (some might say "pain in the ass") nature of my process, and I liked him even more for it.

Still bouncing along in his truck, we headed over to Pulaski Highway toward the tiny community of Pine Island. The whole

area had once been a glacial lakebed that left behind rich, dark soil.
Repeated floodings of the Wallkill River have enhanced the soil's fer-
tility to the point where you could almost stick a shovel in the ground
and it would sprout. Called the Black Dirt Region, it spans 26,000
acres that have been spared from development largely because the
soil, though fertile beyond belief, is too poor for building. Dominique
farms a plot nearby in the summer, selling her products at local
farmers' markets.

We pulled into the parking lot of what appeared to be a convenience store. Inside, it looked like any small-town market except
for the long, gleaming deli case packed with every shape, color, and
texture of smoked meat. And not in plastic packages carrying other
people's logos, either. This was all homemade.

Quaker Creek Store embodies the American dream. In 1939, just
four years before Eugene was born, a man named Stanley Sobkowiak
came to the United States from Poland to work as a garde-manger at
the New York World's Fair. After Hitler invaded Poland he couldn't
go home. He landed a job as a cook in a hotel in Atlantic City. Eventually, his wife and daughter managed to join him.

His wife, Irena, soon grew homesick, so Stanley asked around
and learned about a place in New York that had been settled by Pol-
ish immigrants. That was this place, the Black Dirt region. As luck
would have it, Pine Island's general store and tavern was for sale,
so he bought it. His dream had been to transform it into a high-end
restaurant, but the economics of the region wouldn't support it.
Instead, he built the market's reputation for the very best home-
processed meats.

When Stanley died, the business passed to his nineteen-year-old
grandson, Bobby Mateszewski, who made it his mission to fulfill his
grandfather's dream. He attended the Culinary Institute of America
to study the proper art of being a garde-manger himself, namely an
expert of everything in the kitchen, but especially in the art of making pâtés, terrines, and smoked and otherwise preserved meats. He

plowed a ton of capital into a state-of-the-art basement smoking facility, helped by generous loans from his grandma—who worked at the market every day until she died at the ripe age of eighty-eight.

While they never advertised their business, word of mouth slowly spread, and eventually the store was "discovered" by New York foodies. Folks like Anthony Bourdain and Michael Ruhlman and Bobby Flay have all come, camera crews in tow, to talk with Bobby and sample his creations. Eugene, as it turns out, is one of Bobby's biggest customers. We arrived and were given carte blanche to wander downstairs from room to room.

Men in uniforms looked up at us from various stations. A gleaming stainless-steel microprocessor-controlled smokehouse had just been opened and emptied of its contents. Another room's white tile walls were being hosed down, lending a creepy feeling of a morgue between autopsies. Clearly for Eugene it is a point of pride that his lambs should become sausage at the hands of such skilled people, again reinforcing the idea of hiring the very best and learning from them. Quaker Creek makes thirty varieties of lamb sausage for Eugene. I had assumed they were all based on Mateszewski family recipes, but the truth was a little less romantic.

"I Google sausage recipes," Eugene said. "I pick ones that sound interesting and just have them swap lamb for pork." He shrugged and smiled. "There's no real flavor difference."

The sun was already low in the sky as we headed back to the farm. Eugene had even more sheep tucked away in an outer pasture—ones that hadn't quite lived up to his exacting standards. "You only go forward with the best," he explained. "This is why Saxons are Saxons." Those who didn't measure up were bred with Corriedale or Shropshire "meat" rams to produce big lambs for the market. As dusk approached, it was time to move these sheep back up toward the relative safety of the barn.

A shrill whistle brought Poem, Eugene's Australian Kelpie, from the back of the shearing barn, where the dog had been guarding the gate. Her job was to carry out Eugene's commands in the field. We got in his truck, pulled out onto the road (again, nearly colliding with another car), and quickly turned onto a muddy path along the lower field. He stopped. Just a few days earlier, at this time of day and in this very spot, a coyote had darted across the headlights.

"We'll do it the lazy farmer way," he said, opening the door and letting Poem out. With a single leap she was over the electric fence and into the field. A few bellowed commands from Eugene, and Poem had those sheep lined up and trotting single-file toward the far end of the field. They passed through a gate, which Eugene closed behind them, and ambled back home. It was the most graceful thing I'd ever seen. Mission accomplished, panting and tail wagging, Poem leapt into the truck for the ride back to the barn.

"Good dog," he said, patting her head.

Unlike Stanley Sobkowiak, Eugene has no enterprising grandson in the wings, no clear succession plans for his farm. Both his parents are gone. His younger brother, with whom he was closest, died of cancer six years ago. He has a sister, as well as another brother in California whose wife's politics differ from Eugene's. ("I'm a left-leaning contrarian.") The problem with treating your flock like family is that they can't inherit themselves. They need a human.

"I'm the only one with the memories," he said. "Nobody else remembers the story about the Studebaker, or . . ." His voice trailed off, and we bounced through more muddy ruts. "When you get to this age, you realize just how alone you are. Bettina is probably the person I've known the longest now."

By the time we got back to the barn, most of the light was gone from the sky. The sausage packs were now two rows deep, and the shearers were finishing up their last ewes for the day, squinting under bare light bulbs while Air Supply sang "I'm All Out of Love." More ewes stood quietly outside, their shorn figures looking awkward and small. They chewed and gazed at me. A few were already on the ground, their legs folded up beneath them for the night.

At this pace they'd be done with the ewes by the next afternoon and ready to bring up the rams. They'd seemed mild enough when I met them, but, when challenged, rams are chock-full of testosterone and very reluctant to be undressed. Shearing them involves a much more basic goal: Get off whatever wool you can. Once shorn, they stomp outside for a brief tussle to reestablish dominance before returning to their respective sunbeams. But by the time any of that happened, I would be on the road heading home.

Dominique followed me out to my car.

"The sheep and I just wanted to give you a little parting gift," she said, reaching into her pocket. "It's traveled on my dashboard for years, and now it can travel with you."

Smiling, she held out a tiny plastic lamb for my own dashboard.

CHAPTER 2
DOUBLE BUBBLE BALE AND TROUBLE

DID YOU KNOW THAT, for twenty glorious years, the city of San Angelo, Texas, hosted the Miss Wool of America Pageant? It was a national competition. They flew in twenty-eight Miss Wools from around the country and paraded them throughout the surrounding region in a long caravan of white Oldsmobile convertibles. The crowned winner was given use of a new car for the year, a wardrobe of no fewer than forty woolen garments, luggage in which to carry that wardrobe, and the honor of touring the country in said wardrobe as an ambassador for the American wool industry. Criteria for competing: must be between nineteen and twenty-five years old, have completed at least one year of college, and be able to wear a size ten.

The pageant ended in 1972, but San Angelo is still very much a wool town. Open an edition of the *San Angelo Standard-Times* and you're likely to find news of wool yields and warehouse reports for the season. Once called the Inland Wool Capital of the World, San Angelo is now home to the Texas Sheep and Goat Raisers Association, the Bill Sims Wool and Mohair Research Laboratory at the Texas A&M AgriLife Research and Extension Center, and the Producers Livestock Auction, considered the nation's largest for sheep and lambs. San Angelo is also home to one of the two remaining commercial scouring plants in this country—which is a big deal.

If you plan on doing anything with your wool, whether it's making carpets or long underwear or coffins (yes, they make wool coffins now), the very first thing you have to do is get that wool clean. Straight off the sheep, wool is many things, but "clean" is not one of

If you plan on doing anything with your wool, whether it's making carpets or long underwear or coffins (yes, they make wool coffins now), the very first thing you have to do is get that wool clean.

them. It's full of grease, vegetable matter, dirt, sweat, manure, and anything else the sheep may have rubbed up against over the past year. Once squeaky clean and dry, the wool can be baled and set aside until the carpet factory is ready for you.

When Eugene first began raising sheep, he sent his wool to Adamstown, Pennsylvania, where the Bollman Hat Company—the oldest hat maker in this country—operated a wool scouring and carbonizing facility. (Carbonizing is the process of treating wool with acids to remove vegetable matter. Nobody offers this in the United States anymore.) Bollman closed that line and moved its processing to Texas, and Eugene was left with little choice but to move with them. He had no other viable option on the East Coast. Depending on the year, shipping wool to and from San Angelo can cost up to five times the cost of the scouring itself. Yet even that is still less expensive and more reliable than any smaller-scale scouring operation Eugene has yet to find, although he's always looking.

The region around San Angelo used to produce the largest supply of short, fine wool in this country—the very kind of wool Bollman needed for its hats. Since at least half the weight of dirty wool is lost during scouring, it made economic sense to locate scouring as close to the source as possible. Why pay to ship dirt? (A question Eugene often asks himself.)

Bollman had operated a scour in San Saba, known as the Pecan Capital of the World, before buying the San Angelo plant and moving operations there. It sits on the site of a cottonseed extract plant that was built in 1898 and converted to wool scouring and top-making in the 1940s. Top-making involves an additional step of carding and combing clean long-staple wool into "top" for worsted spinning. That and the carbonizing were both cut for lack of business. Now there is only one top-maker left in the country, which also happens to be the only other commercial scouring plant in the United States: Chargeurs in Jamestown, South Carolina.

I'd never spoken to anyone at Bollman, but Eugene knew them well and volunteered to do the initial heavy lifting. "You should go to San Angelo," he insisted. "It's a place so foreign to Yankees like us." Introductions were made, and a date was set for a visit. Feigning concern for the safety of a single woman driving through the wilds of Texas, my friend Jennifer insisted on flying in from Virginia to keep me company and play Thelma to my Louise.

We headed out of San Antonio at first light, driving northwest into a decidedly flat and scrubby West Texas cattle country. Empty fields were dotted with tufts of cotton as if someone had scattered a box of packing peanuts into the wind. Ornate gates announced ranch after ranch on either side of a long, straight road bleached white by the sun.

San Angelo (pronounced "s'nangelo") sits along the Concho River and has a population of just a little more than one hundred thousand people. It's the county seat of Tom Green County and home to the Goodfellow Air Force Base. A friend of mine was stationed here in the eighties and tells me the whole place stank of wool, especially in the summer. (I would've called it "the fragrance of wool," but, hey, to each his own.)

Bollman Industries sits on a large tract of industrial land just north of town, right next to the train tracks and between Bethel Baptist Church and Acme Iron and Metal. The letters on the sign by the road are faded and peeling, and the only clue to what happens here might be the tall silver water tower.

We parked under ancient pecan trees next to a small brown house marked "office." While I waited for the general manager, Ladd

Hughes, I scanned an office whose decor dated back to the days of *Starsky & Hutch* or *Murder, She Wrote*. A sagging, wood-veneer bookshelf had back issues of publications with names like *Lab Supplies*, *Facility Supplies*, and *Thermal* something-or-other, and several prized copies of a magazine with "Armstrong" in the name. Framed photos hung on the wall: an aerial shot of all the buildings; a black-and-white photo of a man holding a clipboard and standing amid heaps of wool; another of four men in shirtsleeves seated among bales of wool while an older gentleman in a plaid shirt appears to have just said something funny.

Ladd emerged and held out a friendly hand. Eugene had described him as "a soft-spoken and polite Texan," which proved to be entirely accurate. He was tall and slender, with kind eyes. He wore a sweatshirt, old tennis shoes, and jeans with a giant silver belt buckle.

"Shall we?"

He put on a faded baseball cap and led us back outside and toward the scouring plant. As we walked across the dirt yard, Ladd put his hands in his pockets and explained that they'd been having skunk problems.

"It's the pecans they're after," he said, kicking at a nutshell. "Do you have pecans where you're from?"

I shook my head.

"That's a shame. Anyway, we took care of the biggest problem this morning." Why did I suspect the solution did not involve a Havahart trap?

The new scouring building is just a huge metal barn on a concrete slab, with a few small doors and a loading dock at the end. It sits in front of the old scouring building, whose guts were replaced in 2001. That structure is now used for warehousing wool.

The minute we stepped inside, the scent of dirty wool hit me. Then came the sound of massive machines at work, humming, whirring, clanking.

Near us, two men were opening bales of raw wool, pulling out the fibers, and putting them in piles. To one side, I noticed a heap of yellowed wool with green paint on it that was being pulled out of the lot. While ear tags are commonly used, many of the larger Western ranchers will also use paint or chalk branding, especially to identify which newborn lamb goes with which ewe. In theory the paint and chalk are temporary, but traces can still remain in shorn fleece. Paint is one of the main reasons American wool generally sells at about 85 percent of Australian prices.

"They don't do it in Australia, and they don't do it in New Zealand, and they get a higher price at market," Ladd said. "Go figure."

Being from a smaller "flock" farm, Eugene's sheep had no paint, only ear tags, which pose no threat to the wool.

Fibers were being fed into an enormous green metal contraption that looked like the back of a World War II transport truck. It was actually the tail end of what Ladd called the "openers." Everything was concealed behind green metal walls, but inside he said there were two sets of large metal teeth that teased open the fibers and blended them together.

"Shakers" jiggle the wool so that much of the residual dirt falls through a grate at the bottom. The more dirt they can get out of the fibers before they ever hit the water, Ladd said, the less water they need to use. Before they upgraded the whole system and added the shakers, they were using up to three gallons to scour each pound of wool. Now, that number has dropped to between three-quarters and one gallon of water. At three million pounds of wool a year, that's a significant change in water use.

The openers and shakers spanned a few car lengths before making a sharp left and running another few car lengths. At the end, fibers were being mechanically measured and fed onto a conveyor belt leading up to the scouring line. (You'll sometimes also hear them referred to as scouring "trains" because the series of giant metal bowls could, with the right degree of imagination, look like train cars.)

*You'll sometimes also hear them referred
to as scouring "trains" because the series
of giant metal bowls could, with the right
degree of imagination, look like train cars.*

From where I stood, all I could see was a maze of pipes, pumps, and valves. Hidden behind them and running the length of the line were giant inverted steel pyramids, pointing downward but never actually touching the ground, like angular udders. With all the commotion above, you had the feeling of standing under a ride at an amusement park, complete with occasional splatterings and drizzles of mystery liquids. But step back and you'd see thick wisps of steam wafting lazily upward, as if someone just lifted all the lids on an industrial-sized restaurant steam table—but instead of chicken cacciatore or broccoli in cheddar sauce, the six giant stainless-steel tanks were filled with hot, wet wool.

Until 2001, Bollman had been operating with 1940s equipment (Ladd kept referring to it as "the old Sargent line," and I nodded sagely as if I knew what that was). The new Andar system they imported from New Zealand (another approving nod) allows them to run up to three times more wool with less labor and less water. The plant employs thirteen people.

While they prefer to scour at two thousand pounds per hour, the system can be cranked up to as high as twenty-five hundred pounds per hour if needed—which translates into being able to wash and dry up to twenty-five thousand pounds of wool per workday. Eugene's entire clip would take just an hour to scour.

"Of course we can dial it down to a thousand pounds per hour if we need to," Ladd said. I gave another knowing nod, pretending we all knew one thousand pounds was the magic number. It is, however, the minimum amount they can accept. "Without at least one thousand pounds," Ladd explained, "you don't have the critical mass to keep the wool moving forward." At last, I could give a nod of genuine understanding.

He led us up metal open-mesh steps to the top of the scouring line. Before me unfolded the most glorious mechanical contraption I'd ever seen. It was indeed a long train-like structure of six car-sized stainless-steel tanks filled with very hot water. The first three had soap for the wash, and the second three ran clear for the rinse. Like food being digested by an earthworm, the wool moved from bowl to bowl as one nonstop mass.

As it marched forward, it passed through a pair of roller pressers that squeezed out as much liquid as possible. "It's set for twenty tons of pressure after the first wash and the last rinse," Ladd explained. "All the others are set at ten tons." I'd given up nodding and was just trying to keep up with my notes. (I'd asked Jen to do the same, but she was too distracted by Ladd's belt buckle.) The roller pressers help prevent dirty water from moving with the wool into the next tank, allowing Ladd to run the system longer before having to drain and refill. While the old Sargent system had to be drained every day, this one has a series of self-cleaning mechanisms and can go a whole week before needing to be drained.

Every once in a while Ladd would lean away to spit—into one of the open runoff tubs, toward the wool making its way to the dryer, over the edge of the train, anywhere. I assumed it was chewing tobacco. His aim was impressive.

Waste water is disposed of in the San Angelo sewer system following strict EPA guidelines, and Bollman pays the city a pretty penny for the privilege of doing so. I sensed that this was a source of frustration for Ladd—not that they had to play by the rules but that foreign competition didn't.

"Eighty percent of U.S. wool goes to China or India for scouring," Ladd said. "They have no labor or environmental regulations like we do here." He shook his head. "Some plant in India could run their pipe down the middle of a street and nobody would say a thing. They can scour and comb for less than half of my wash cost. You can't compete with that."

Ironically, at $0.55 per pound, Bollman is by far the cheapest option for Eugene. Boutique scouring operations in New England, the kind smaller fiber farms must use, run upward of $5 per pound. For a thousand pounds of wool, that's the difference between $550 and $5,000—or, for Eugene, it's the difference between a viable business and a nonviable one.

As busy as Bollman seems now, it used to be busier. As recently as 2005, they ran in twenty-hour shifts processing eight million pounds of wool. A devastating draught in 2011, declining wool prices, and global competition from China and India have more than halved that number. Today, Bollman operates in ten-hour shifts and processes three million pounds a year—of which only one hundred thousand pounds goes toward Bollman hats. Now that Mohawk Industries (the second largest carpet manufacturer in this country) has moved everything overseas, the plant is kept afloat primarily by Pendleton, Crescent, and Woolrich—all of whom still need to import wool because the United States doesn't produce enough of what they need.

Ladd kept walking us down the line. At each tank I noticed little bowls with gurgling streams of runoff being funneled into more pipes below, presumably part of the system's self-cleaning function. The first stream looked like bubbly dark coffee, whereas by the last bowl it had lightened into diluted iced tea. Ladd explained that the fiber spent about seven minutes in each bowl, and the majority of the dirt and grease was caught in that very first bowl.

Meanwhile, the wool was constantly pushed forward by the most mesmerizing part of the whole system: fierce-looking metal claws called "harrow rakes." They dipped into the woolly water at a perfect ninety-degree angle, pushed the contents forward, and then lifted out of the water to return to their original position for another dip, and another, and another. Since back-and-forth agitation felts wool, the rakes never reversed direction—they only dipped in, pushed forward, and then lifted out. It was hypnotic, like watching the taffy pull at the Santa Cruz Beach Boardwalk.

We were still standing on the raised catwalk running alongside the tanks. Glancing back on the floor below, I noticed a tall green thing that looked like a beer keg. It was their newest toy: a lanolin extractor from France. It had been in operation for only a few weeks. Water from the first tank was constantly pumped into the extractor, where centrifugal force caused much of the grease to rise to the top and the residual grease to cling to the dirt and sink to the bottom. Thus cleaned, the water in the middle was pumped back into the scouring system. Their goal was to achieve 5 percent lanolin extraction from that first wash. So far, they've been able to fill one 420-pound barrel with wool grease every day, which they sell to companies that further refine it into lanolin for the cosmetics and nutritional supplement industries. That income helps them keep scouring prices as low as possible.

Ladd said workers would often dip a finger in the grease and rub it on whatever needed softening, healing, or waterproofing. "Usually a boot," he said. The antibacterial and antifungal properties of lanolin are designed to keep the sheep's skin healthy, which makes it rather perfect for our skin, too. Picking up on my desire to add a 420-pound barrel of wool grease to the project, Jen shot me a "no" shake of the head.

After that last twenty-ton press, the wool moved up a conveyor belt and into the dryer, another recent upgrade. Their old flat dryers took longer because the heat covered less surface area. Now the fibers move through a series of drums, allowing for faster and more even air circulation and surface drying.

We walked around to the other side of the dryer, where gorgeous white fluffiness puffed out of a chute and onto a long table. Two people ("those are the pickers," Ladd said) were pulling the wool open, fluffing it, and moving it forward. Every once in a while they'd pull something out and throw it into a barrel, presumably a contaminant that the scour didn't get.

Three flat metal bars protruded from the top opening of the dryer chute. Ladd explained that they were moisture monitors. "We've gotta have at least twelve percent moisture in the wool as it comes out of the dryer, or else it'll build up static in the blower tubes and we'll get a jam in the ducts." Based on what those monitors sense, the whole line can be sped up or slowed down.

"The tricky part," he said, "is that we can't go higher than fourteen percent moisture or we'll get a wet spot in the wool, and once it's baled, it'll rot."

From here, wool was pushed into a large tube that sucked it into a series of ducts running up and across the ceiling. It reminded me of the old vacuum tube systems department stores used to have. Soon enough, one of the pickers left his station and climbed a ladder up high onto a catwalk. He opened a little door along the chute, and the inside was packed with fluffy white wool. He gave it a push, then another push, and the wool moved along again. Ladd had stepped in to help with fluffing and sorting but kept an eagle eye on the man until he got back down safely.

Up high I saw that the chutes ran through a big noisy metal box. "Those are the dusters," Ladd explained. Inside were two chambers with a flat piece of mesh lining the bottom and a powerful vacuum sucking out residual dust from below as the fibers moved past. Like a turbocharged winnower.

At long last, the clean wool tumbled down into the bale feeder. Through a little glass window I could see fibers landing inside a chamber like microwave popcorn. Once they reached capacity—they try for 630 to 650 pounds—the top was closed, fibers pressed, bale secured with four bands of baling wire, and popped out the other end, where it was wrapped in thick blue plastic and loaded on a forklift.

They were midway through a job for Pendleton, which runs some 1.5 million pounds of wool through the line every year. A wall of bales was already stacked floor to ceiling, marking that morning's work. Suddenly my 676-pound bale felt a little silly, and yet that's why I was here.

"Can I see my bale?" I asked.

Ladd gave an amused smile and said, "Sure."

He walked us over to a vast area that was mostly empty, just a few dozen bales stacked in various piles. "It's usually very full," he explained, "but we're just waiting for wool season." As soon as shearing picked up in earnest, the eighteen-wheelers would be pulling in fast and furious. Everything about wool—its harvesting, its processing, even its wearing—is seasonal.

My bale sat in a cluster with the other small-run customers. Another bale of Eugene's wool sat on top of it (aha, so he'd been holding out on me!), and to its left were two other bales marked "Elsa." In addition to being a friend and mentor, Elsa Hallowell is a pathbreaker in the yarn world. She's one of the first people to successfully market and sell breed-specific wool to the craft market. I loved that our bales got to sit next to each other. It felt like good luck.

Having seen the true scale of their operations, I was trying to play it cool with Ladd. But as soon as he stepped aside to take a phone call, Jen snapped a quick picture of me hugging my bale. Here it was, both my vehicle for learning and the instrument of my potential downfall. Only time would tell. I wondered if this was how people in arranged marriages felt when they finally met their new spouse. Or was I taking things a little too seriously?

We were admiring a bale of dark wool when Ladd returned. It belonged to the wool buyer for the clothing company Ramblers Way, he explained. Begun by the founder of Tom's of Maine, Tom Chappell, Ramblers Way was manufacturing wool clothing sourced entirely in the United States.

"I just can't understand why anyone would want to buy wool that couldn't be dyed," Ladd said. While knitters and spinners prize colored fibers like these, the commercial market—the kind that sends Ladd 1.5 million pounds of wool a year—sees them not only as undesirable but downright dangerous. Just a few dark hairs in a batch of brilliant white Merino could ruin an Armani suit and all the fabric that had been made for it.

They're an expensive liability, nothing more. Jen asked Ladd what kind of wool it was, by which she meant maybe Rambouillet or Merino or even Targhee, and he kept answering, "black." Though even he agreed it was of excellent quality.

Just as I was getting comfortable with the noise and the smell and the machinery and the bales of wool, Ladd was opening a door back to the outside. A massive wind tunnel from the ventilation system did its best to keep us inside, but alas, it failed. That was too fast, I thought. I wanted to run back to the first door, hold up a ticket, and beg, "Can I go again? Please?"

Walking to my car, I was struck by the tenuousness of it all. By the unstoppable tide of globalization, by what once was and what now remains, by how much an entire country and industry depend on this one operation.

I asked Ladd if there were any hope for wool, in the face of everything he'd told me.

"Oh sure," he said with a smile. "People using it."

CHAPTER 3
INFILTRATING BIG WOOL

AMERICAN NATURALIST JOHN BURROUGHS gave us the optimistic adage, "Leap, and the net will appear." On the day I reached out to Ladd about my visit to his scouring plant in Texas, the ghost of Burroughs (who grew up on a farm just two hours north of Eugene's) did me a favor. Ladd said he was free every day the week I'd proposed except Friday, when he'd be in San Antonio for the ASI convention. The very same San Antonio that I was flying in and out of, and where I'd be staying.

ASI is shorthand for the American Sheep Industry Association, the chief advocacy group for more than 88,000 sheep producers around the country. Launched in 1865 as the National Wool Growers Association, it was the first national livestock association in the country. Before cattle, before pigs or poultry, it was all about sheep. Correction: It was all about wool.

If you're producing wool in any significant quantity in the United States, if you run a mill or manufacture woolen products, if you operate a wool-testing lab or a scouring plant or are a broker, chances are you belong to ASI or have a very good reason why you don't. Anyone who belongs to one of the forty-five state sheep associations is also automatically a member of ASI.

It feels odd to call farmers "producers," but it's their preferred term. I once made the mistake of saying "sheep farms" in a talk out west. A woman who'd spent years on a giant ranch in Montana pulled me aside afterward and whispered a warning. They don't like it when you call them "farms" out here, she said. *Charlotte's Web* took place on a "farm." Cute little East Coast hobby flocks like Eugene's, those are "sheep farms." West of the Mississippi—where the big money is, where most of ASI's energy is focused, where most of our wool comes from—you'd better call them "ranches" and "sheep producers" if you want them to do business with you.

Once a year, all these card-carrying sheep ranchers and producers and professors and chemists and veterinarians and scientists and brokers and mill managers and dyers and, yes, even some farmers, all come together for four days of meetings and roundtables and keynotes and cocktail parties.

Until now, my familiarity with ASI had been from a polite if somewhat intimidated distance, like a Hollywood extra might view the Academy. This is Big Wool, the domain of giant mills and factories and ranches with tens of thousands of animals. I was just a yarn reviewer and an occasional knitter, a consumer of wool yarn so far downstream from their universe that I might as well be from another planet. But the timing was too perfect to pass up.

First, I had to crack ASI. Most trade groups I've tried to join required everything but a DNA sample and a reference from my fifth-grade teacher. But all I had to do for ASI was fill out a form, send money, and book an extra night at the hotel. I think they figured that only serious people who were in the business would willingly spend four days listening to talks on mycoplasma ovis research, crop insurance for ranchers, or the objective measurement industry. It's not a show the public generally wants to crash.

Until now, my familiarity with ASI had been from a polite if somewhat intimidated distance, like a Hollywood extra might view the Academy. This is Big Wool, the domain of giant mills and factories and ranches with tens of thousands of animals.

The event took place at a hotel along San Antonio's River Walk, a sort of Mexican colonial-style subterranean Pirates of the Caribbean complex with tourist-filled boats and roaming mariachi bands. On street level, your view of San Antonio is rather blank, with lots of sidewalks and buildings, but if you find stairs and trot on down, you're in a completely different world.

The conference schedule looked daunting. There were no lectures or classes, just mostly council and board meetings and roundtables. What I could and could not do was a mystery. My plan, therefore, was to keep it simple. I would slip into the hotel, get my name badge, and wander through what was advertised as a show floor. I would do a few laps, take notes, perhaps snap some pictures for everyone. I'd pick up a pamphlet or two if I was feeling brave, and then I'd reward myself with a margarita down by the river.

All the other trade shows I'd attended had giant screens blaring glitzy tech ads or colorful walls of yarn and needlepoint canvases. I didn't really know what to expect from ASI: sheep-related things? Hopefully I could blend into the crowd and nobody would notice me. That isn't the healthiest attitude, I'll give you that. But it's where I was at the time.

An escalator brought me down to a mezzanine level where people were milling about. Mostly men, and a few women. The first thing I noticed was the cowboy hats. Then the shoes—cowboy boots mostly. And the jackets—casual wool blazers, often plaid. The men stood in clusters, staring at their feet while they talked, their fingertips tucked precariously into the tops of their jeans pockets.

It brought to mind something Eugene had told me during the shearing. He said it's rude to stare a sheep directly in the eyes. Sustained eye contact will make them nervous. They much prefer to stand close and occasionally let their gaze graze the side of a neighbor's face before turning back to the ground. I don't know who got the habit from whom, but that's exactly what the ASI people were doing.

I collected my badge and swag bag with "Eat American Lamb" emblazoned on the side and went to find the show floor. It turned out that I was standing right in it. This was the extent of the show floor. Not even a dozen exhibitors. They were pitching things like ear tags, fencing, and polypropylene-free bale bags. Fine exhibitors, all. But I was done in ten minutes.

It quickly became clear that the real activity was happening behind closed doors, or in those impenetrable conversation clusters in the mezzanine during breaks.

An extreme case of shyness overtook me. I couldn't figure out a way to break in. I kept circling the mezzanine, snapping pictures, smiling like I knew what I was doing, while growing more convinced that this was going to be the extent of my experience at the ASI conference. I dreaded having to admit my failure to the people back home. Would it cost me my Master's of Yarn-Making degree?

Then I spotted a sign for a meeting: "Wool Council Producer Session."

The room was small, with a band of tables down the middle and name cards at each seat. To the left, a row of chairs had been set up for onlookers.

It was the annual meeting of the Wool Council, a fourteen-member group whose ultimate mission is to improve the American wool industry and promote the use of American wool worldwide. They oversee the research, quality control, and marketing activities made possible by the federally funded Wool Trust.

I desperately wanted in this room.

Like a stray dog at a kitchen door, I kept circling back, peeking in, hoping for an opening, and then retreating.

At a certain point I began to annoy even myself, so I went to the registration desk and asked the kind woman what, exactly, my badge enabled me to do. Could I, for example, attend the Wool Council meeting?

My plan to remain invisible was immediately thwarted as we were asked to go around the room and give our names and where we were from.

"That's an open meeting," the woman said with a smile. "Just go on in!"

By the time I went back, a full thirty minutes after the meeting was scheduled to start, they'd put several more rows of chairs around the perimeter of the room and people were finally starting to sit down. I slipped inside and grabbed a seat just as they called the meeting to order.

My plan to remain invisible was immediately thwarted as we were asked to go around the room and give our names and where we were from. I recognized nobody by sight, but some of the names were quite familiar. I'd read their books and articles and reports when I was researching for *The Knitter's Book of Wool*. Here they were, in the flesh, sitting with me in this room. I marveled at the prospect of getting to spend hours listening to these people.

Everybody was here—the professors, the farmers (excuse me, *ranchers*), the wool buyers, the mill managers, the wool graders and testers, everyone involved in large-scale wool production in this country. They came mostly from western states, such as Utah, Colorado, Wyoming, South Dakota, Texas, and the like, with one person from Massachusetts. My own "Maine" got a few curious glances, but nothing more.

They did meeting-ish things, approving minutes and going over financials that made no sense to me. Then we met the winners of that year's Make It with Wool contest, a youth-centered competition sponsored by the same groups that had organized the Miss

*In 1923, when American wool was in
its heyday, the university established
an entire department dedicated to
wool research.*

Wool of America contest all those years ago. People came and went, and proceedings were frequently interrupted by a symphony of cell phone ringtones.

But when Bob Stobart stood up and began talking, we hushed. In the world of wool research, this man is a legend. He is the last wool faculty member in the University of Wyoming's animal science department, and he was retiring. For reasons both budgetary and, some suggested, political, the university had chosen not to refill his post. In fact, they'd condemned the entire wool research lab and were forcing him to dismantle all the equipment and dispose of its library.

In 1923, when American wool was in its heyday, the university established an entire department dedicated to wool research. It was nationally renowned, even helping the USDA develop federal standards for wool fiber. When Stobart came on the scene, he taught three classes on wool each semester. "I haven't done that in fifteen years," he told me during the break, after I'd mustered the courage to introduce myself. "Now we're lucky if we have one class per semester. Not on wool, even, but on sheep rearing." There's just not enough money in it anymore, he said. Agriculture isn't profitable like an MBA program or football team. "Plus, the next generation just doesn't want to do the work."

The wool library is no small thing. Stobart's predecessor, and the first to head the department, was an even greater legend named Robert Burns. During his tenure, Burns cataloged every single publication dealing with wool, with physical fiber samples dating back to the

1800s. Before I could pull a Norma Rae and hop onto a table with a big "SAVE WOOL" sign, he reassured me that the library would be preserved by the university's special collections department. Eventually they plan to digitize it and make it available online, which will be a gold mine for wool geeks.

But the equipment? The mini scouring train, the carding and processing machine, and the French combs? They all had to go. If Stobart didn't find a home for them, they'd be sold for scrap. In the meeting, Stobart walked us through all the prospects that had come and gone. Currently a minimum-security prison was his most viable option for the equipment. The prison administrators liked the idea of being able to train inmates to run equipment and generate revenue. "On a positive note," he said, "I suppose they do have a captive workforce."

Talk of the Wyoming wool lab underlined a deeper fundamental reality that was becoming all too clear: The American wool industry is not growing. No significant new money is being invested. The infrastructure is aging, the workforce is retiring, university programs are being shuttered. Nobody will be there to train the next generation, and the next generation doesn't seem to have any desire to be trained.

Talk turned to ASI finances, and suddenly Big Wool became . . . not quite so big. Every year, ASI receives $2.25 million from the Wool Trust, formally known as the Wool Research, Development, and Promotion Trust Fund. Authorized by Congress in 2000, the Wool Trust is funded from tariffs charged on imported wool and wool textile

---

Talk of the Wyoming wool lab underlined a deeper fundamental reality that was becoming all too clear: The American wool industry is not growing.

products. While ASI receives some additional funds from membership dues and the government, it would fold if the Wool Trust disappeared. Imports hurt the American wool industry. Yet, ironically, without them, the American wool industry's only advocacy group would not be able to operate. How's that for a catch-22?

With a little digging, I discovered that this import tariff system has been funding the wool industry for quite some time. In 1954, just as synthetics were really beginning to punch a hole in the wool market, Congress passed the National Wool Act. It created a price support program for domestic wool and mohair producers, and it was funded by, you guessed it, tariffs on foreign imports—but back then it was to the tune of more than $200 million a year. According to Eugene, ranchers had little incentive to improve the quality of their wool since they were paid for it no matter what. When the incentive payments ended in 1995, they were gutted. Wool production soon plummeted.

By the time the Wool Trust was created in 2000, significant damage had been done. Every few years, the funding comes up for renewal, and everyone holds their breath. How long the funding will continue is anyone's guess.

According to a recent economic impact study, the American sheep industry adds $5.8 billion to the U.S. economy—yet its voice in Washington, D.C., is almost inaudible. The Pharmaceutical Research and Manufacturers of America spent $25.8 million on lobbying in 2017. By comparison, ASI's entire lobbying budget hovers around $175,000, all from member dues. Wool outreach programs? Just $200,000. Are you starting to see the problem?

Back in the meeting, we moved on to other numbers. Global wool production is at a seventy-year low, we were told. While it seems to be holding steady, all the production, sales, and export projections are still following a downward trend—and even those numbers were given with a cautionary, "If we're lucky." I don't know if I'd expected better news, but I certainly wasn't getting it. If anything, I felt like

I'd trekked upstream only to discover that the dam keeping my town safe was actually aging and riddled with cracks.

At last, we were told about a tiny growth spot that exists for the industry: smaller farms that are cropping up and raising specialty flocks. Farms like Eugene's. Farms where "every sheep has a name," which got a chuckle from the group. (For the record, Eugene's sheep all have numbers—which I've never heard spoken so lovingly as when Dominique called to her ewes on shearing day.)

The tone in the room suggested that they considered these smaller farms rogue operators—liabilities, even—that clearly didn't care about or fully understand sophisticated issues of fiber quality and breeding. In addition to sheep, these operators often also raised—and here was a palpable shudder—alpaca.

I'd been writing about yarns from these small farms, from rare and unusual sheep breeds, breeds that the "regular" wool channels won't even acknowledge as of importance, for decades. The fiber arts world prizes the very colored fibers that ASI considers a contaminant. We'll pay ten times what these farmers would ever get on the open market for their wool. The real issue for us is simply that of scarcity. You're lucky to find a farm—yes, farm—with more than one hundred of these more interesting, unusual sheep breeds. Since numbers equal power and visibility, those smaller players get very little support or recognition from ASI.

The question was asked, "How can we bring them into the fold?" But I was left wondering if we were the ones who needed to bring ASI into our fold. There in San Antonio, all the attention was going to the handful of big producers, customers, and deep pockets keeping ASI afloat, leaving the countless smaller producers and customers and pockets to fend for themselves, despite the fact that they had potential to carry the future.

Everyone in the room seemed to be so intent on keeping the big buyers for that name-brand clothing company or for the Department of Defense happy that they had lost sight of an even bigger urgency:

making people want to wear wool in the first place. Ladd said it himself: The only hope for wool was people using it. Without demand,
there will be no product.

Instead of paying a branding agency to create glossy "wool is
great!" brochures to hand out at trade shows, ASI should be plow-
ing its resources into broad public campaigns to raise the profile of
wool, the desirability of wool, its innate attractiveness and magic,
among the actual humans who'll be wearing it. Instead, it would take
the American Wool Council another four years to set up an Instagram account.

If consumers don't show an interest in wool, companies will
have zero incentive to make anything out of wool—which means they
won't be buying wool from American producers. It's that simple. Was
I the only one seeing this?

Remember when I said that global wool production was at a
seventy-year low? There was one outlier: the United Kingdom. In
2012, wool production in the UK actually increased by 6.2 percent.
Not coincidentally, these numbers came two years into the UK's
Campaign for Wool, a massive program initiated by His Royal High-
ness the Prince of Wales to raise public awareness of, and appreciation for, wool. Here in the United States, ASI is the largest possible
voice for wool, and it's not being used.

The meeting adjourned. There was a reception at a nearby restaurant, but I'd had enough for one day. I needed to find a quiet place
to sit and think. Out a back door I went, down some stairs to the
water. I walked for a while, passing mariachi groups and women
in high heels teetering perilously close to the river's edge. I found a

---

*If consumers don't show an interest in
wool, companies will have zero incentive to
make anything out of wool.*

table just as the sun set. I skipped that margarita and went straight for a gin and tonic.

I'd wanted to come away with a sense that things were going to be okay, that the adults in the room knew about the problem and were actively engaged in fixing it. Instead, I felt that ASI needed help, and that I—we, the people who make with wool and wear it out into the world—could actually be part of the solution.

I didn't know how much, if anything, I could accomplish with my 676-pound bale, but I was more determined than ever to try.

CHAPTER 4
MOVING BODIES

GETTING THE BALE TO MAINE was an adventure. It turns out a good 50 percent of yarn making has zero to do with making yarn and everything to do with simply moving wool from place to place. Unless you have your own end-to-end wool-processing plant, you'll need to figure out how to ship from the ranch to the scourer, from the scourer to the mill, from the mill to the dyehouse, and from the dyehouse to the warehouse. Then you have to get the product to your customers, or to the store that will, in turn, sell it to the customers.

Shipping freight is like entering the Bermuda Triangle. Each shipper will give you dramatically different quotes. Change the origin ZIP code and you could easily knock $400 off the bill—or add another $1,000. It made no sense to me. Then you have to specify the NMFC for your item. That's the National Motor Freight Classification, a standard that catalogs eighteen traditional freight "classes" or commodity types for interstate freight. And the numbers do not go from one to eighteen, as one might expect. No, they start at 50 and run rather randomly to 500 depending on item density, handling, storability, and liability. An item with an NMFC of 50 easily fits on a pallet, weighs about fifty pounds per cubic foot, and is very durable, say, something like sandbags. At the other end of the spectrum, an NMFC 500 item could be bags of feathers or ping-pong balls. Turns

---

Shipping freight is like entering the Bermuda Triangle. Each shipper will give you dramatically different quotes.

out, the bale's NMFC is 70. Oh, you also have to note whether you're shipping a carton, drum, pallet, or skid—none of which applies to a bale. It goes on.

Even after the bale was in motion, there were hiccups. The bale went MIA between Vermont and Maine for three days, prompting fears that it had slipped off the back of the truck as it crossed the bridge from New Hampshire to Maine and kerplunked to the bottom of the Piscataqua River. Or, worse yet, maybe Eugene and Ladd had orchestrated a hoax and were, at that very moment, toasting each other on a beach in Guatemala. Eventually the bale arrived safe and sound. Apparently things can go on temporary walkabouts when you ship freight.

Now that it had arrived from the scouring plant in Texas, I would need to open my bale to divvy up smaller amounts of wool for each mill. This skill is not frequently taught in school. Nor is there a *What to Expect When You're Expecting a Bale* book for expectant bale-openers. But I did know someone who'd opened bales before: Anne Bosch and her husband, who operate the Blackberry Ridge Woolen Mill in Mount Horeb, Wisconsin. She was on my short list of potential mills for the project. I wrote her for advice on how to get this thing open, ending with a naive but sincere plea, "Is it true they explode?"

She wrote back right away.

The wires will require wire cutters. The long-handled ones work best because they give you better leverage. You should wear protective eyeglasses and make sure no one else is near. The wires can fly fast and hard. We leave most of the plastic bag on the bale to help keep the wires under control, which works most of the time. The bales are about 2.5 x 2.5 x 6 feet [.75 x .75 x 1.8 m]. If all of the wires are cut at one time, it could double or triple in volume. Even if you don't cut all of the wires, it can sort of bow out in the middle like a banana. Make sure the floor around it is clean.
Have fun!

I wasn't liking the sound of this. What if I hurt myself? What if I went blind? What if it really did explode?

I am not naturally athletic. I have chopped firewood just enough to prove that I can, but otherwise my ideal form of physical exertion involves walking to a place that serves tea and toast. I wasn't liking the sound of this. What if I hurt myself? What if I went blind? What if it really did explode? People were expecting a story, and "I asked a stranger named Joe to open the bale, so he did, and now it's open," wouldn't cut it. I had to do this myself.

At the Ace Hardware store on Route 1 in Falmouth, Maine, a friendly man named Dennis lumbered over and asked if I needed help. Why yes, I did. I told him I needed some wire cutters, protective eye gear, and gloves. As he mulled over my request, I added, "I'm opening a 676-pound bale of wool today."

His eyes grew big. Clearly this was exciting news for Dennis. He wanted me to be prepared.

Dennis found me the right pair of bolt cutters ("Wire, you say? Any idea what gauge?"), gloves (their smallest so-called work gloves for women were bright pink with "TuffChix" emblazoned on the side), and eye protection. I also got a drop cloth to cover the exploded bale, a Swiffer to clean up the floor around it, a box of quart-sized bags for mill samples, and garbage bags so I could begin divvying up the fiber. I honestly thought I could just dump hundreds of pounds of scoured wool into garbage bags and send it on its way. All the while, Dennis told me about his career in construction, and then his career in law enforcement, pointing to each scar on his body and explaining how it got there. He also told me all about his leather-working hobby, pulling out his wallet for show. Dennis was all for me opening this bale of wool.

Car loaded with supplies, I set out for the old Pepperell Mill Campus in Biddeford. I had also packed a camera and tripod so that my survivors would have video footage to show the authorities when they were asked, "How the hell did that happen?"

The bale was in Biddeford because my friend Pam Allen, who owned the yarn company Quince & Co. at the time, was doing me a great big favor. Pam had teamed up with three others to purchase the assets of the bankrupt JCA dyehouse in Massachusetts and move everything to Biddeford, where they had just relaunched it as the Saco River Dyehouse. They had leased a huge space on the ground floor of Building 13-1, the very same building and floor where the old Pepperell Mill dyehouse used to be. At that point they still had far more space than they needed, so Pam subleased a portion for the Quince warehouses. She, in turn, had more than she needed. I had a bale, so we struck a deal.

While the Pepperell Mill complex has since become a warren of lofts and offices and restaurants, much of it hadn't yet been developed. It had the feeling of a haunted indoor playground the size of a football field, with ancient creaky wood floors and tall narrow windows, many still covered with wood or even bricks. When they'd moved into the space, Pam told me they'd found a gold mine of 1960s office furniture, much of which they kept for their own use.

While Quince was a major customer of the dyehouse, it certainly wasn't the only one. No walls separated Pam's yarn inventory from racks upon racks of freshly dyed yarn, some for her, some for her competitors. Sometimes her competitors came to tour the dyehouse or talk colors, staring at the Quince shelves as they did so.

The other dyehouse partners quickly began showing a keen interest in my bale, especially Claudia and Ken Raessler (who would soon become the sole owners). Before the dyehouse, they had raised alpacas while Claudia worked as a lawyer and Ken as an anesthesiologist. When I arrived with my wire cutters and TuffChix gloves, Claudia intercepted me. She peppered me with questions about this woolly presence that had been deposited in their midst. She'd already reached in and pulled out a sample of fiber. "It feels very nice," she said. She wanted to know my plans for it. Where would I be shipping it? Did I know how? Which mills would I be using? What kind of yarn would I make? Did I need help?

My immediate response was to evade all her questions. Who was this person trying to horn in on my bale? But more than that, I couldn't reveal my plans because I didn't have anything fleshed out yet. I had a vague idea of how it could work, but my plan was to let each action inform the next. Otherwise, how could I correct my course as I learned new things along the way?

Claudia drifted off, and I stood studying my bale. They'd put it on a wooden pallet and tucked it between two pillars along the main thoroughfare between the Quince warehouse and the dyehouse. The plastic had several big gashes in its midsection, the exposed fibers darkened by what I hoped was just dirt acquired during freight transport. I hoisted myself up onto the bale and asked Pam's assistant Jerusha if she'd mind taking my picture. When I got off the bale, my hands and my jeans were covered in a fine black grime.

"Oh yeah," she said, "you'll probably want to keep your stuff covered around here." Good thing I got that drop cloth.

Looking at my bale again, I had no idea just how much this thing would explode, or in which direction. But if it did, or if anything went awry, it could block access to the dyehouse. Not a good idea.

Jerusha ran off to get a hand-operated forklift she'd seen among the dyehouse equipment. We wiggled it in place, fiddled with the lift mechanism, and successfully moved the bale to a more explosion-friendly resting spot at the end of the Quince shelves facing into the dyehouse. From here the bale could explode all it wanted, although I hoped it wouldn't.

Floor swept and equipment ready, there was no more delaying the show. Time to begin. I donned my protective eye gear, slipped on the TuffChix gloves, grabbed the wire cutters, and tiptoed toward the bale. Anne had advised that I keep the plastic on while I cut the wires to keep them from flying into my face, and I realized this would also help contain the wool. Clever.

I positioned the mouth of my wire cutters over the first wire, took a deep breath, and pulled the handles together. From within the bale came a small "pop" that made the warehouse floor jump. I reached in and snipped the next wire. The boom was louder, like gunfire. People started coming over to see what was going on, fully expecting a construction crew to be doing demolition. I welcomed them, saying I could use witnesses to tell the emergency crews what happened. Standing at a safe distance that only made me more nervous, they watched and advised, none of us ever having done something like this before.

There were four visible bands of wire, each band composed of two wires. I could feel the force holding those wires in place. With each wire I cut, the pressure of the compacted wool was transferred to the remaining wires, making the next snip of the wires cause an even louder boom that made the floor shake. The plastic covering the bale grew taut; the tape securing it creaked ominously. It really did sound like a large building on the verge of collapse. By the time I reached the final wire, I was getting scared. This was the point of no return.

I took another deep breath, adjusted my protective goggles (which had begun to fog from all the excitement), and clipped that last wire. I jumped back. The bag creaked and groaned, and then the noise stopped. Nothing. We all stood and stared, wondering what to do next. I'd cut all the wires, I'd freed the fibers from their bondage, but they still hadn't exploded. How was I to cut open the bag so that the fiber would move in the direction we needed, without doing myself or anyone else bodily harm? Great theories were discussed. We debated whether a vertical or horizontal slash in the plastic would be most effective. I settled on a plan: I'd cut from the farthest end, where all the plastic had been tightly folded over and taped shut

*With one arm behind my back and
the other extended like Zorro, I lunged
forward and jabbed at the plastic, then
quickly retreated.*

like a birthday present. It had more plastic through which the fibers could travel before hitting the floor.

With one arm behind my back and the other extended like Zorro, I lunged forward and jabbed at the plastic, then quickly retreated. Nothing. I did it again. And again. And again, at which point the bale finally began to creak like a redwood preparing to topple. Jerusha got a scared look on her face, pointed at something, and ran away, while Lisa, another onlooker, started shouting, "Go around! Go around!"

I must have knocked something over, tipped something in such a way that the whole building, or at least the long, heavy metal shelf behind me, was on the verge of collapse, taking down the next and the next like a very fatal game of dominoes, with me buried beneath it all. Just as I turned to retreat, the wool burst from its plastic and oozed out into the open like sausage being squeezed from its casing.

We all stared at the wool, mouths open, silent. I crept closer, unsure if more was getting ready to blow. But it was still.

When I finally regained my composure, I asked Lisa what that whole "go around" thing was about. "You almost gave me a heart attack."

"Oh," she said with a shrug, "Jerusha was about to walk in front of your camera."

The most peculiar thing about the fibers was how they'd formed flat layers, almost like a mille-feuille pastry or the pages of a book. I'd never seen anything like it before, but then again, I'd never opened a bale of wool before, either. The fibers were definitely sheepier than I'd expected—shorter and more jumbled and with little bits of hay

> *It was so simple and pure and soft and lively, like a puppy. Or 183 puppies, which is the number of sheep whose coats contributed to this bale.*

and other vegetable matter. Would a carding machine get it all out? Is this how all commercially scoured fiber looks before it goes to the mill? Or had I pinned my entire public standing on something that, in actual fact, wasn't all that great? I'd promised to be completely honest with people, but could I be *that* honest?

I pulled out a tiny tuft and began playing with it. The fibers were extremely tender, baby-like. As I teased apart the clumps, the fibers started to wake up. I took a lock and ran my pinched fingers along it. The fibers stretched and stretched and stretched, then sprang right back to shape when I let go. It was irresistible. I pinched and stretched again, and again. It was so simple and pure and soft and lively, like a puppy. Or 183 puppies, which is the number of sheep whose coats contributed to this bale. And they were telling me that everything was going to be okay.

Soon I'd be back to repackage the fiber in four bundles so they'd be ready to go when I had decided what my four mills would be. But for today, for now, both the bale and I were exhausted. I tucked it in and bid it good night.

CHAPTER 5
READY TO ROLL

MY LITTLE BALE had gained a fair amount of notoriety in the knitting world by now, and people were eager for a peek at *The Bale*. Here it is! Reach in, have a touch!

During a dyehouse tour, one woman did reach in and help herself to a touch, which she then stuffed in her pocket. This she admitted to me a few days later after cornering me at a local event. "I took it to my spinning group." She narrowed her eyes and leaned in as I inched backward. "It's not that good."

She stood back and eyed me proudly, as if she'd figured out the answer to a puzzle and was waiting for the prize.

I took an instant dislike to this woman. Not because she'd stolen from me, and not because she'd insulted my wool, but because she'd managed to hit me in a vulnerable spot. I have no memory of what I actually said to her, but "you're right" wasn't it. I just knew it was time to repackage that bale and get the wool in motion. Once I saw how it performed at the mill, I'd be able to judge its quality for myself.

Luckily, Claudia at the dyehouse was no stranger to shipping fiber. She had the bags, the manpower, and the shipping connections. In fact, she'd just shipped four hundred pounds of alpaca to Tennessee.

"Believe me," she said the next time I was at the dyehouse, "I've been trying to get my mind around this shipping business for some time now."

She promptly produced an enormous rectangular cloth bag with flaps at the top. Aha, so this was a bale bag. I remembered Eugene telling me about these during shearing, how the bigger ranches used pneumatic bale pressers to pack hundreds of pounds of wool into perfectly shaped blocks. Up close, it just looked like a big square sack. She set it out on the floor, and while I contemplated exactly how we were going to do this, people from the dyehouse began to appear.

Brian, a new hire who grew up in the mill and was thrilled to be back in it, brought over a tall cardboard box into which they could put the bale bag, like a frame, so that it'd stand up and stay open while we filled it.

I lifted the drop cloth and tenderly pulled aside the plastic on the opened end of the bale, like a doctor examining a patient. Brian and Claudia looked at me, and then at each other.

Brian stepped in with a box cutter and made two broad, fearless slashes in the plastic. While I gasped, he ripped it open so they could get at the fiber. Easy there! Too fast! Slow down!

Then I noticed a brown area in the fibers, like copper, or rust. An alarm sounded in my brain. Was that . . . water damage? Was my bale not only bad wool, but rotten too? It wasn't a big spot, and the fiber around it still looked and felt fine. I decided to pretend I hadn't seen it.

Claudia called over two more people from her crew, who introduced themselves as Jeanne and Whitney.

"What do you need?" Jeanne asked, rolling up her sleeves.

"You want this in there?" Whitney asked.

Not even questioning what we were doing or why, they jumped right in and started helping. They stuffed and stuffed and stuffed that bag with armfuls of wool until they thought we'd reached 168 pounds—my bale, more or less divided by four. Brian rolled over a small scale, and they dragged the box onto it. The verdict? Nowhere near.

By now the bag was able to stand up on its own, so they removed the cardboard box and kept stuffing.

During a lull in the conversation, Jeanne told me how she had worked in the office of this very mill for thirty years, back when WestPoint Home manufactured Vellux blankets here. For everyone

*Then I noticed a brown area in the fibers,
like copper, or rust. An alarm sounded in
my brain. Was that . . . water damage?
Was my bale not only bad wool, but
rotten too?*

at the dyehouse, this building was a lucky find. Most of the other mill buildings they'd looked at hadn't been upgraded or improved in decades, while this one had been maintained until WestPoint Home shut it down in 2009.

"So you must remember the carding machines and the spinning frames," I said wistfully, but she shook her head.

"Oh no, that was long gone. These were all synthetic."

She marveled that we were standing in the same spot where they used to dye the blankets. I asked if it was hard for her to be back in a place that had so much history for her, and she shook her head. "I'm just so happy to be back here and see the space being used." She paused. "It's home."

By now we were sure we'd reached our weight, so they pulled over an even bigger, ancient Toledo scale that normally stands in the back loading area next to the women's restroom.

Bingo! One bag done.

While our backs were turned, however, the bale appeared to have replenished itself. For all that we'd removed, we hadn't made a dent in this thing.

"You want us to do another one?" Brian asked.

The conversation shifted, and then Jeanne chimed in, "So are we doing another one?"

Not until they'd asked three times did I realize that they actually wanted to do more. So we got out a second bag and began stuffing it. They got faster.

How do you keep bale bags closed, pray tell? Do you use a staple gun, or perhaps duct tape? Nope. You use bale fasteners, of course.

We did a third bag in what seemed like no time at all. I felt bad telling them to stop before the bale was empty, but I needed to keep some wool accessible in case mills asked for samples. Plus, it was all going too fast. At this rate the whole project would be done in a month, and then where would I be? We stopped there, and I thanked Brian and Jeanne for their time.

The adventure wasn't over. I had to seal the bale bags shut and get them ready for shipping. How do you keep bale bags closed, pray tell? Do you use a staple gun, or perhaps duct tape? Nope. You use bale fasteners, of course. Because such things exist. Made of galvanized wire by Maspro in Australia, they're a bit like a half-open paperclip but with viciously sharp edges. They have to be sharp so they can puncture the bale bag and hold it snug.

Claudia and Whitney set to work folding over the top flaps, inserting a fastener into the edges, pulling the top taut, and then slipping the other end of the fastener into the body of the bag. They added two more fasteners along the flap, and along its sides, to keep everything snug.

This particular bale was going freight, so it'd need to be further secured. "I have just the thing," Claudia said, and then disappeared. A few minutes later she returned, pushing a new contraption in front of her. They had stocked up on all sorts of gizmos for the dyehouse but hadn't even opened the wrapping on this one yet. It was a strapping machine.

I was suddenly overcome with a wave of joy at the utterly fresh, unknown adventure of it all. This was already such fun, so random, and it was entirely of my own creation. I loved not knowing and then walking through the process of learning, of finding out how things are done. And I loved that fate had placed me here, standing with two smart, strong women, learning how to master a machine we had just encountered.

As if reading my thoughts, Claudia smiled and said, "If I'd asked you a year ago if you'd be standing here trying to figure out a strapping machine . . . ?" I laughed and replied, "If I'd asked you a year ago if you'd have a dyehouse?"

We pulled out the instructions, read them multiple times, considered the matter carefully, and proceeded to wrap our first wool bag with two rounds of sturdy black strapping. It would then be placed on a wooden pallet, tightly wrapped in plastic, and shipped off to a mill far away—a mill whose identity was still undecided.

This whole letting-other-people-into-my-business thing was new territory for me. I'd been a fiercely solo operator for the past thirteen years, defending my editorial independence and rejecting anyone's attempts to attach strings to my work. But here, I had to accept that I couldn't do it all myself. I'd already hired my trusted friend Jane Cochran to manage the master spreadsheet of all my Great White Bale Explorers and Armchair Travelers, and to respond to their emails in a timely manner. Which she did beautifully, although we never did get the spreadsheet quite right.

Today I really needed help again, and Claudia was happy to offer it. The deal we struck was this: She would help me ship my wool (this and the other bags), and in return I would spread the word about a grant campaign she was working on. She needed help getting people

I was suddenly overcome with a wave of joy at the utterly fresh, unknown adventure of it all.

to vote, and I had access to tens of thousands of people through my online writing. I'd never made such a tit-for-tat bargain before, but I justified it by telling myself I didn't agree to promote her campaign; I just said I'd help publicize it.

But watching the genuine entertainment my bale had given the people in the dyehouse that day made me realize something else I'd never considered before: Asking for help doesn't always mean making other people miserable. In fact, if you're doing something really fun, it's almost selfish not to share.

CHAPTER 6
BARTLETT BOUND

MY WORK WOULD HAVE BEEN much easier if this project had taken place before 1775. I would have handed my bale to a farm family and watched them turn it into fabric. The children would tease open the fibers and prepare them for spinning. The women would spin the fibers into yarn, and the men would weave that yarn into fabric. That's how textiles were made. By hand.

Things changed dramatically in the 1770s, with the invention of the water frame and the spinning jenny—two devices that automated some of the yarn-spinning process. Then in 1779, Samuel Crompton, a weaver who was frustrated by the limitations of those two inventions, took what he did like—the moving carriage of the water frame and the drafting rollers of the jenny—and incorporated them into a new invention he called the spinning mule.

He gave it that name not because it looked like a mule or was powered by mules or because a mule once saved Crompton's life and he wanted to show his gratitude, but because the machine was a hybrid of two others, just as the mule is the hybrid offspring of a female horse and a male donkey. It quickly became the standard, and by the time Richard Roberts patented further improvements in 1825 that made the mule fully automatic, the industrial revolution was off to the races. Eventually the mule was replaced by something that gets the job done twice as fast. Today, the spinning mule is a rarity. Only one remains in commercial operation in the United States. Lucky for me, it is in Maine, just a few hours from where the bale was sitting.

In 1821, Ozias Bartlett opened a mill along Higgins Brook in the tiny town of Harmony. It was powered by a single water wheel. By

1907, the mill was listed as a maker of knitting yarns with two sets of cards, two looms (marked "idle"), and 144 spools (mills advertised their capacity by the total number of spools on all their spinning equipment). The mill also offered dye services and sold direct to the public. Even as late as the 1940s, the mill operated in two shifts with a staff of twenty in constant production. Today, Bartlett spins just 140 pounds of yarn a day and employs seven people.

I knew I wanted to get inside this mill. Rumor had it that Bartlett was a very tough nut to crack for custom work. The owner had a reputation for being gruff, if not downright curmudgeonly. I'd always imagined a crotchety Old Man Bartlett standing in the mill doorway waving a rusty Civil War musket and yelling, "You get off my property!" This is rural Maine, after all.

It turns out, Old Man Bartlett (whose real name was Russell Pierce and who was a perfectly fine person, I'm told) had since sold the mill to a retired New Hampshire firefighter named Lindsey Rice. Lindsey and his wife, Susan, had for decades operated a farm, raised sheep, and brought their wool to Bartlett for spinning. On more than one occasion, Lindsey had helped Russell fix a rope drive band that had broken and needed splicing. After a particularly urgent rescue run to the mill with his wife—on their wedding anniversary, no less— Lindsey asked Russell if he'd ever thought of retiring. Talk turned to numbers, and Lindsey and his wife found themselves the proud new owners of a very old mill.

There was only one problem: They lived in New Hampshire, and his wife had no desire to abandon her proximity to Boston and New

---

I'd always imagined a crotchety Old Man Bartlett standing in the mill doorway waving a rusty Civil War musket and yelling, "You get off my property!"

York for life in a tiny Maine town in the middle of what could easily seem like the epicenter of nowhere. They put their farm on the market anyway, the idea being to downsize. For the seven years it took them to sell, Lindsey trekked up to the mill and back every week, sleeping on a cot in his office. Though they still maintain roots in New Hampshire, they have since bought a little place in the area. But at the time of my project, Lindsey was still commuting—and his weekly commute took him right past the dyehouse in Biddeford.

Being extremely phone-averse, I emailed Lindsey my pitch for the project. I told him that I had 168 pounds of scoured Saxon Merino to be spun into a heavy fingering-weight two-ply yarn, delivered either on cones or weighed hanks, depending on their preference. (I'd been told this was the kind of information mills liked to see, and I wanted to impress him with my professionalism.) As for timeframe, I said, "as soon as you have an opening in your schedule," praying it wouldn't be autumn of 2036. And then I added the potentially prickly part: I needed to be at the mill for some portion of the project. I went on to explain the bale, the journey, the goals, the people who would be reading along and getting the yarn. The number of witnesses to any potential failures or shortcomings on his part. Oh, and there was no practice wool; this was it. Mess it up, and the project is toast.

I'd been warned about timing. My wool mentor, Elsa Hallowell, who has been creating Cormo yarn for decades, put it best: "The textile industry has taught me to be persistent in nudging people, and has also taught me that the nudging may accomplish nothing. Mostly I just float along at whatever speed the river is flowing."

On the day I contacted Lindsey, though, the river was running fast. He called me right away and said yes. I believe, "Sure we can!" were the exact words. I'd caught them just as they were finishing up with "the naturals," and they could get it done in two weeks. I was stunned.

Just as Bollman scours from fine to rough each week, mills also tend to run in color and fineness cycles. Dark green crunchy wool

*In yarn as in life, there are good neps
and bad neps. There's a time for cream of
rice cereal that you could drink through
a straw, and there's a time for lumpy,
wholesome, steel-cut oatmeal.*

fibers would be an obvious and undesirable contaminant in a fine white run, while a fine white fiber would disappear and pose few problems in a darker blend. The more colors you have, the longer the whole cycle from light to dark takes. With sixty-five shades total in Bartlett's line of house yarns, the wait could have been very long indeed. Considering that some people have waited months bordering on years to get their colors, I was very lucky.

Besides having the last commercially operating mule in this country, Bartlett is unique for another reason. While many mills spin wool that has come from thousands of miles away, Bartlett has remained local to the core. Its farm program lets sheep farmers in the Northeast drop off their annual clip and receive a percentage of that amount back in spun yarn. Farmers pay nothing out of pocket and get yarn that, while not 100 percent "theirs," is distinctly local. Some families have kept a running tab at the mill for years, dropping by whenever they need something—like $20 bills from an ATM, only they're skeins from the yarn bank. Those who don't want any yarn in return get a set price for their wool instead. Working this way, the mill gets some sixty thousand pounds of local wool each year. Some of the spun yarn goes into sweaters and blankets Bartlett manufactures in New England; the rest goes into the yarn.

This clever wool-sourcing arrangement comes at only one price: fineness. The sheep breeds that thrive in the cold, damp climate of the Northeast tend to grow longer, stronger fibers—hefty British-style ones that some might call "crunchy" or "crisp" or "robust." Merino and other super-soft premium breeds struggle the farther north you raise them. For Eugene to have such a fine flock in New York is a rarity, and it's largely due to his adherence to the original breeding standards for Saxon Merino—ones for sheep that also thrived in Saxony before their move to Australia.

Another special thing about Bartlett is the range of colored yarn they sell under their own name. Every year, Lindsey takes advantage of discounted shipping rates on empty trucks leaving Maine to send his wool to Chargeurs in South Carolina for scouring. That wool is then shipped to Philadelphia, where G. J. Littlewood & Sons dyes it into fourteen base colors. (Littlewood is equipped to dye wool before it's spun into yarn, a process called "stock dyeing.")

Back in Maine, using color-blending recipes that have been handed down for generations, Lindsey and crew artfully combine those fourteen base colors into the sixty-five shades of Bartlett's own yarn. These heathered colors and rugged New England fibers combine to form an exquisitely old-school yarn. While the equipment could, in theory, spin anything from cotton to asbestos, it's been perfectly calibrated to suit the fibers of New England. This meant that my wool—my shorter, much more fragile fiber—was in for a challenge.

"I have to warn you," Lindsey said on our first call, "it might be a little neppy."

Neps are like little pills or lumps. In yarn as in life, there are good neps and bad neps. There's a time for cream of rice cereal that you could drink through a straw, and there's a time for lumpy, wholesome, steel-cut oatmeal. Accidental neppy yarn is a tragedy, but done on purpose, the results can be a very good kind of lumpy and wholesome. I needed to see what the wool from my bale would do.

Within a week, a green pickup with YARN vanity plates backed up to the dyehouse loading dock. Claudia emailed me a blurry cell

I was seeing real New England now.
A Breezy Acres Motel advertising
air-conditioned rooms, a trout pond,
and paddleboats.

phone picture of the bale bag, the truck, and a beaming Lindsey. A few days later, I headed up to Harmony, a place I'd never been, to watch my very first yarn be made.

It's a fun drive, the kind of time-travel experience that's harder and harder to come by. Past Augusta, I left the Maine Turnpike behind, then the strip malls and Starbucks drive-throughs. Soon enough I was bouncing north on a two-lane road that ended in Canada. I was seeing real New England now. A Breezy Acres Motel advertising air-conditioned rooms, a trout pond, and paddleboats. A vinyl-clad American Legion building where you could take your state driver's license exam. The back side of a drive-in movie theater with a "no hunting" sign in the ticket booth window.

A heavily laden logging truck passed me heading south. Then another, and another, each spraying a muddy mist on my windshield. Ahead, fantastical clouds of steam billowed from the Somerset Paper Mill, now owned by South African conglomerate Sappi and one of the area's largest employers, producing 725,000 metric tons of paper and 525,000 metric tons of pulp each year.

I passed through the elegant old mill town of Skowhegan, birthplace of the first woman U.S. Senator, Margaret Chase Smith. It's also home to the New Balance shoe factory and one singularly unremarkable Thai restaurant. Recently, Skowhegan has also gained notoriety in the country's regional artisan bread movement after the old jail was bought and transformed into a grist mill. Maine Grains and the Maine Grain Alliance offer inspiring tales of rebirth and regeneration of a local economy.

It was spring, and the heavily rutted side roads were all posted with fluorescent orange "Heavy Loads Limited" signs. The frost heaves were bad that year, turning even the main road into a series of roller coasters best taken slow if you didn't want to go airborne.

Just past the old Athens Grange Hall I saw a tiny sign for Harmony. Not a proud "Welcome!" sign, but a small green road marker that indicated a right turn. A mile or so down an even bumpier side road, I reached a cluster of old wooden-frame houses along a river. This was downtown Harmony.

I spotted the tower first. A tall, weathered gray box attached to an equally weathered gray building. In the muddy bleakness of Maine's early spring, it had a sinister look. The place reminded me of the Stephen King story "Graveyard Shift." It's set in an old Maine textile mill with terrible rat problems and a maze of tunnels that run beneath it. Of course, people start dying. And because it's Stephen King, the tunnels lead to a cemetery where a massive and completely horrifying rat creature devours unsuspecting humans at night.

Remembering this story made me briefly consider turning around and getting out while I still could, but reason prevailed. Closer, I saw new trucks parked along a cheerful blue outcropping of buildings opposite the mill. Lights were on, and as soon as I got out of my car, Lindsey bounded out the door and extended a hand. "So you found the place!"

He was jolly and energetic, as if St. Nick had shaved his beard, lost a few pounds, and moved to Maine to start a mill. Immediately he demystified the place for me. We walked toward the mill, which looked less sinister by the minute. He explained that we were looking at a "new" mill building constructed in 1921, after the original 1821 structure had burned to the ground. They'd gone all out with the new mill, giving it state-of-the-art things like a poured concrete foundation, three-phase electric power (unheard of at the time), a flame-retardant metal roof and metal-clad siding, a water tower fire-sprinkler system, and even a telephone, steam heat, and flush toilets.

But by 2007, when Lindsey bought the mill, business operations had started to lag. If he hadn't come along, he estimates that the mill would've lasted only another year before having to close. It had no website, no email, not even an answering machine. All the books were maintained by hand in a big ledger, and invoices were typed on one of five typewriters.

Maine can be a very tribal place, especially in smaller towns. The arrival of an outsider was not universally celebrated. His modernizations were stressful for some. When he presented the office manager with a cordless phone, she eyed it suspiciously and asked, "What is it?" (She has since left.) Lindsey persisted, adding answering machines and email and QuickBooks and, yes, cordless phones. But the heart of the operations, the spinning of wool yarn, remains unchanged.

As we got closer to the mill, I heard the hum of equipment from inside and the rushing of water from the stream that had once powered the mill and still flows alongside it. I remembered a question I'd wanted to ask. I had heard that yarn straight from the mill needs to be washed to remove any residual spinning oil and perk up the fibers. Did the mill still offer any washing or dyeing services?

"You see that river?" he asked.

(Actually, neither of us could. It was on the other side of the building.)

"The EPA comes twice a year to make sure we aren't dumping anything in it. Even our toilets have to run their pipes under the building, under the road, under those houses, back and beyond . . ." He kept pointing.

"Off to a cemetery with giant man-eating rats?" I joked.

He turned and smiled. "Oh, did you know they shot *Graveyard Shift* here? In our basement!"

While I was processing this new bit of information, he opened a small, weather-beaten door and beckoned me inside.

There's a smell that a good, wholesome, old-fashioned wool yarn has. It's pungent and spicy and woolly in a way that can be intoxicating. It's not just the smell of sheep or barnyard. Yes, it's some of that, but it's also the scent of lanolin and the special oil that is sprayed on fibers to tame static and lubricate their journey through all the equipment. I followed Lindsey inside, and that fragrance—at full strength—hit me like a big sheep-shaped pie in the face. My brain went into sensory overload. I looked around the sunny, wood-filled space with gorgeous, old, perfectly preserved, well-oiled, still-operating mill equipment. It was like I'd been shrunk to the size of a pinhead and dropped inside my mother's Singer Featherweight sewing machine. It was heady and overwhelming. My ability to ask smart questions, take notes, and document the visit with photos and videos was severely impaired.

Still talking and not at all sensing my distress, Lindsey pulled me along on his well-rehearsed mill tour. We started in the basement so we could see where the wool came in, was tossed into a sealed room, and was blown around to be blended and opened. The walls had blackened over time from all the lanolin and dust, forming a perfect surface for past workers to leave their mark. Rodney Giles had written his name in tidy script. A "Randy was here" had been modified to say "wasn't." In big, bold letters, Earl declared his love for Alice.

Lindsey led me to a "duster" that circulated air through the fibers and vacuumed the debris into a separate bag. He likes to run fibers through the duster twice to make things easier on the spinning

---

There's a smell that a good, wholesome, old-fashioned wool yarn has. It's pungent and spicy and woolly in a way that can be intoxicating.

equipment. He opened a clear plastic bag to show me the debris they'd gotten from my wool. It looked like beach sand but with the consistency of sawdust. I was surprised by how much was still in the wool after it had been scoured. He told me that even more would come out when it hit the carding machine upstairs.

An old wooden conveyor belt covered with thin metal spikes grabbed the fibers and led them into the "picker," where fierce metal claws teased open the fibers and prepared them for carding. On their second pass through the pickers, brass-tipped nozzles sprayed a fine mist of oil over them, like that spritz of oil in the pan to keep vegetables from sticking.

"It's a water-soluble, non-petroleum-based cotton conditioner," he explained. "Hair conditioner, really."

The fibers are then blown through ducts up to the mixing room on the top floor. We walked up creaky wooden stairs that had worn down in the middle from decades of use, past a yellowed piece of paper on which was carefully handwritten, "Not Responsible for Injuries to Visitors," past a cartoon outline of a sheep drawn in white chalk, past a faded blue ribbon from the St. Louis County Fair, to the top floor where the cards and spinning mule reside.

With its exquisite shapely form, its metal tracks and steel wheels and long row of orderly spindles (now numbering 240), this mule is a work of art. A hand gear starts and stops the mule and looks exactly like the one that San Francisco cable car drivers use to operate the cars. Taken together, it was the most stunning machinery—ancient, elegant, fierce, and graceful—that I had ever seen. Ironically, this equipment that gives this mill its most historic quality is also its newest, made in 1948 by Johnson & Bassett of Worcester, Massachusetts.

On the other side of the room is the carding machine, a glorious yet still functional relic built in North Andover, Massachusetts, by the Davis & Furber Machine Co. in 1919. This machine's sole purpose is to take clean wool and tease open the fibers, draw them all into the same direction, and give any remaining dirt or vegetable matter a chance to fall out.

The carding machine is made up of many, many cylinders, each coated with fine wire teeth rather like industrial-grade cat brushes. Each cylinder is a different size and rotates at a different speed in such a way that the fibers are constantly pulled from one cylinder to the next to the next. The wool enters as clumpy pillow fluff and emerges as a diaphanous sheet of fibers that is then gathered like a veil, lifted overhead, and then laid mechanically on a second set of cards at a ninety-degree angle, so that everything is blended and aligned twice as evenly. Technically, it's a two-breaker woolen system with a camel-transfer in the middle and a finisher at the end.

The finisher was the best part. At the back of the whole thing— which has the size and imposing presence of two circus calliopes parked head to head—the sheet of fiber is split into ninety-six little strips, each the width of a pinkie finger. These strips are fed through the most crucial part of the whole thing: the "rub condenser." Wide green rollers move side to side in opposite directions as the strips are drawn between then, rubbing the fibers together so that they can hold their cohesion when draft and twist are applied on the mule. At this stage it's called "pencil roving," and it forms the basis for the woolen spinning system.

Up to this point, everything had been shown to me while the equipment was off. All surfaces were covered in a layer of wool fluff as thick as a stack of pancakes in places. To prevent drafts, milky plastic had been stapled over all the windows. My wool had been running through the cards when they shut them off, as had the yarn on the mule, the spindles only partially full. That sense of life frozen at a crucial moment, paired with the antique surroundings, ghostly fuzz, and equally ghostly light gave the whole setting the feeling of Miss Havisham's mansion in Dickens's *Great Expectations*. The anticipation was killing me. I finally asked Lindsey if we could start up the equipment. I'd come to watch yarn be made, after all.

Over the next two days, Lindsey showed me everything. He started up the cards so I could watch the fibers draw from one cylinder to the next, opening and aligning into a sheet of beauty. I could laugh at the comical "waa-waa-waa" sound made by the rub condenser, its aprons drunkily tottering back and forth while spitting out strips of wool.

Best of all, I got to watch the mule. If there is one thing I wish for you in this world, it is a chance to witness a spinning mule in action. It is a beautiful ballet of fiber and machinery that mimics the movements a handspinner makes when using a walking wheel. The spool of ninety-six pencil roving ends is moved off the cards and over to the mule, where it's placed on a fixed head called the "creel." Each of those ninety-six ends is fed through rollers and attached to a corresponding bobbin on a carriage. Set in motion, this elegant chorus line of bobbins pulls away from the creel, traveling some five feet on a metal track, all while each bobbin is rotating and applying twist to the roving.

During this "draw stroke," all is in a tremulous state of suspended animation. Tiny tufts of fiber pop into the air like woolly fireflies, while the yarn itself vibrates like the strings of a harp.

The spell is broken when the bobbins stop spinning. A long metal "faller" wire pushes the freshly spun yarn down to bobbin height, and the carriage jerks back another foot or so to take up any slack. Then it begins its return trip to the creel, a process called "putting up," winding freshly spun yarn onto each bobbin as it travels.

The dance repeats itself four times a minute—the carriage traveling on its track, the fibers making another dance midair, then

---

If there is one thing I wish for you in this world, it is a chance to witness a spinning mule in action.

another clamp of the wire, another jerk back to take up tension, and another putting up. From every angle—and I tried them all—it was absolutely glorious. Lindsey began leaving me places, at subsequent stations, while he went about his business.

The minute one of the pencil roving strands runs out, the whole process is shut off. All remaining unspun pencil roving ends are ripped off the other spools and tossed in a bin for re-carding. Meanwhile, the completely full bobbins of freshly spun yarn are put in another bin and dropped through a chute to the next wonderland, the second floor.

That's where I met Cheryl, a cheerful brunette in bright white New Balance sneakers, who wasn't sure if she was the second or third generation of her family to work in the mill. She showed me how they took yarn from the mule bobbins and rewound it onto the bobbin required for the next step: plying, or as they call it, twisting. They had rows of pegs set up to hold mule bobbins, many of them endearingly reinforced at the base with layers of duct tape.

Their twister dates from 1928, and its sole job is to twist together two (or more) strands of spun wool into a plied yarn. The trick is to calibrate the twist so that it renders a balanced yarn, which you won't be able to know right off the bobbin because the twist requires time to set. They had it down to a science.

After the first round of twisting was done, I followed her to the skeiner, where she hoisted forty bobbins of plied yarn atop the frame. With practiced speed, she tied a tail end of yarn from each bobbin onto one of the long wooden slats that formed a cylinder running the length of the machine. Picture the slats of a park bench forming an open cylinder that runs for twenty feet and can collapse into itself like an umbrella—necessary for getting the skeins off the frame. Once everything was ready, she pulled a lever that set the cylinder in motion. It spun and spun and spun, taking the yarn from the cones and winding it into large bands, or skeins (sometimes also called "hanks"). This particular piece of equipment was so old, they'd had to put wood blocks under all the legs to raise it a touch—people are taller now than they were one hundred years ago.

Cheryl ran the machine until the cylinder had made the precise number of rotations that would deliver a skein weighing four ounces (113 g). While most mills now work in the metric system and deliver skeins in grams (usually fifty or one hundred), Bartlett remains loyally calibrated to the Imperial system. Cylinder stopped, Cheryl then made her way with lightning speed down the line, snipping each end and tying it loosely around the skein in what looked like a single motion. When she'd finished, she started all over again, this time retrieving the original end of each skein, all forty of them, and tying them around the skein and knotting the end. She did this all while chatting and without missing a beat.

"As a knitter," she said, "I really envy this run. It's so springy!"

She closed the cylinder's umbrella frame just enough to be able to pull the skeins to the end, where she loosely twisted them into groups of five and carried them in giant puffy armfuls to a waiting scale nearby. Each bundle had to weigh exactly ten pounds, which meant they were spinning, plying, and skeining a perfectly consistent yarn. If it was off, something had gotten miscalibrated and would need to be checked.

I held my breath while she looked at the scale. She smiled and nodded. "Yup! Ten pounds on the nose!" She wrote it in an old three-ring notebook, then marked and numbered each bundle with a manila tag.

Not all of Bartlett's yarns end up skeined. Some go onto big cones for weavers and machine-knitters—including the Massachusetts company that makes classic crew-neck sweaters for Bartlett. They'd approached a nationally known outdoor retailer about carrying the sweaters, but the rep told them that their customers wouldn't pay $75 for a New England wool sweater. (To which I say true: They'd pay $175.) Bartlett does a swift business selling direct and wholesale, and these sweaters are very popular in Japan.

At the end of my second day, I asked Lindsey when he thought everything might be done. It was already April, and people were eager to get their hands on some yarn.

"I should have the rest ready for you by . . ." He paused. "Thursday?" he said.

Cheryl shot him a wary look and reminded him that someone was going to be out that day. At that time, they were producing about five hundred pounds a week with "two bodies," as Lindsey had put it.

"Friday." He paused. "Well, I want to be safe here, so let me say Monday." I waited.

"No, Tuesday," he said, nodding. We settled on the following Thursday, and he walked me out to my car.

I asked Lindsey if it bugged him that some people considered his mill more of an out-of-the-way museum than a working business. He laughed and shook his head, and then he recited the names of other equally busy textile manufacturers in the area. Harmony is not in the middle of nowhere, he insisted. In fact, quite the opposite. I got the sense that he had big plans for the place. My hunch was correct: In just five years he would be opening a small wool-scouring operation and representing Maine in a Made in America product showcase at the White House.

All this time I'd been eyeing the wool like a hungry child on a tour of a bakery, looking but not touching. When Lindsey suggested I take a few bundles home to tide me over until the rest was done, it finally hit me that all this work I'd watched, all that yarn being made, was mine.

I tenderly placed six bundles of fresh yarn into the car, resisting the urge to buckle them in with a seat belt, and we said goodbye. Even before Skowhegan, I started to get a whiff of the yarn. By Augusta, the whole car was full of that intoxicating perfume—the

Mulespun yarn is like a child who has been given a solid foundation—a thorough carding and cohesive rubbing into pencil roving—before being allowed to run free and gather life experience.

residual lanolin and sheep and spinning oil combined. It got stronger and stronger until even I, one of the greatest fans of the smell, had to crack open the windows. As if he'd secretly placed a tracking device in the yarn, Lindsey called just then: "I'm just checking to make sure you haven't passed out from the wool fumes?"

That night I held a skein in my hands and waited for the usual reaction—the ho-hum ennui, the conclusion already written in my head without using the stuff. There was nothing but an eagerness to snip that knot and get my hands into the wool. I cast on a random number of stitches and began to knit. And knit. And knit. My hands were unable to stop.

Even before I had a chance to wash out the spinning oil and let the fibers relax, the yarn was already thick and spongy and succulent, with an extraordinary degree of loft and bounce that are the telltale signs of mulespun yarn. The neps didn't seem so much like pills as they did intentional texture, like a thick chenille bathrobe.

It seems counterintuitive that fibers pulled and drafted and twisted over such a long distance, to which so much freedom has been given, would actually be so airy and even. Yet it is. Mulespun yarn is like a child who has been given a solid foundation—a thorough carding and cohesive rubbing into pencil roving—before being allowed to run free and gather life experience. After the twist has been applied, the yarn is all too happy to wind its way back onto the spindle, telling its family everything it learned that day.

Modern spinning frames remove that wide expanse of exploration, and the subsequent storytelling, by doing all the drafting and twisting over a very short distance. The yarn is lovely, as we'll soon see. But it isn't as special.

What was supposed to be a little test square got longer and longer until I realized I had the beginnings of a cowl on my hands. The fabric had a plush, sheepy presence that instantly calmed me. It brought me back to shearing day on Eugene's farm. I'd gone into the pen and was sitting with the waiting ewes. The most outgoing of the bunch—a sweetheart named 126—slowly trotted over and began sniffing me. After she'd deemed my hand safe, she let me reach up and rub her cheek. My fingers inched into the deeper wool along her neck, and I began to scratch. She stopped chewing, her eyelids fluttered, and she leaned into me. We sat quietly like this for a long while before Dominique returned and the spell was broken. Working with this yarn, made from her wool, evoked that very same sense of almost otherworldly connection.

For the first time since I couldn't remember how long, I knew I was right where I was supposed to be, doing exactly what I was meant to be doing—and I couldn't wait to see where the wool took me next.

CHAPTER 7
THE STRADIVARIUS OF SALVAGE

THAT "NEXT" TURNED OUT to be the town of Mount Horeb, Wisconsin, approximately twenty miles west of Madison. There sits a small, unassuming mill that has produced some of the country's most extraordinary woolen-spun yarn since 1988. It's that little Michelin-starred restaurant tucked down an obscure country road miles from any big city, but instead of pea velouté and assiette of lamb, it serves yarn.

You won't find this mill processing ten-thousand-pound orders for national brands; that's not its style. Those in the know will nod their heads when you mention Blackberry Ridge Woolen Mill. They'll inevitably say something good about the owner, Anne Bosch. She knows wool, she knows yarn, she knows her equipment, and she will not allow anything to leave her hands until she deems it perfect. Which she will signal with a reluctant nod and, if you're lucky, the words, "It's okay."

Part of Anne's secret is that she has hands-on experience working with the material she creates. She knits. Which is rare for someone who operates a mill. Even more remarkable? She does all her work on salvaged equipment that she manages to play like a Stradivarius. She's a master. The equipment she uses—a Whitin spinning frame—is the type that eventually rendered the mule obsolete. I wanted to understand the evolution of spinning. I needed someone who was willing to take the time and walk me through it. Anne could do it. I just had to convince her.

The mill was deep into the dark portion of the light-to-dark color cycle when I wrote. Anne said they'd be shutting everything down and cleaning the cards soon. They only do this twice a year, so my timing was good. But first, she needed a sample of my fibers. She wouldn't commit until she'd tried them out for herself. If I didn't mind the cross-contamination with darker fibers, could I send her a sample so that she could quickly run it through the cards?

I boxed up a few pounds of my wool and shipped them off, fingers crossed. Within days, Anne emailed me a collection of pictures. To the untrained eye, by which I mean mine, they all looked the same. They showed three sheets of white wool presumably coming off the cards, all with little tufts of pills in them. A caption explained that the top one was her "house" wool, the middle one was mine "on gear eighteen," and the bottom was also mine on gear eighteen but with "weights having been added to the feed box to make the card run lighter." I had no idea what this all meant, but I loved how serious it had already become, and it made me even more eager to work with Anne. In her previous life, she had been a biochemist and spent the bulk of her career as a study director at a contract laboratory. ("Which is why I try not to eat fast food or take any prescription drugs," she later told me.) Everything she does with wool has a similar scientific precision to it.

Anne said she'd love to spin my wool, but with one caveat: The yarn wouldn't be perfectly even. There would be some neps because the wool was so fine and the fibers were a touch short for her cards. Having just created the yarn equivalent of oatmeal on the spinning mule at Bartlett Yarn, I was not opposed to more neps. I suspected that Anne's definition of "not perfect" was quite different than mine. Caveat given, she agreed to the project. I gave Claudia at the dyehouse the go-ahead to send Anne our second bale bag of wool, and I bought my plane ticket.

I'd last been in Madison to speak at the Madison Knitters' Guild, which is one of the largest in the country. In fact, Wisconsin and Minnesota could vie for the position of the most knitterly state, perhaps because of the high percentage of early immigrants from northern

European countries. They brought their exacting and prolific knitting traditions with them. The cold climate also helps.

Wisconsin has a leg up in this imaginary competition because it was home to the most influential knitting figure of the twentieth century, Elizabeth Zimmermann. She and her husband, Arnold, emigrated from England in 1937, eventually settling in Wisconsin, where they raised a family. Arnold spent the rest of his life working as a brewmaster. Elizabeth went on to design knitwear and then write her influential Newsletter. She became a yarn importer, running both a mail-order company and publishing house. She appeared on public television and hosted an annual "camp" that has become multiple camps, all of which continue today under the deft and loyal leadership of her daughter Meg Swansen and grandson Cully. While everyone likes to call her the Julia Child of knitting, I prefer to think of Julia as the Elizabeth Zimmermann of food.

Meg still lives in her mother's schoolhouse in central Wisconsin, but a few times a year she makes the trip down to Madison to see her daughter, Liesl, and granddaughters Renata and Cecilia. The luck of the bale prevailed yet again. I emailed her on a lark, and before I knew it, we had an early-morning date to meet up at a Panera in Madison—with the family in tow—and caravan out to the mill. Liesl's daughters were old enough to be trusted around mill equipment, though not quite old enough for it to hold their attention for more than an hour. I was overjoyed to have Meg's company for however long she could stay. It felt like a royal blessing.

We drove west through farmland that turned to increasingly steep hills and valleys. Our road got narrower until the final turn put us on a dirt road leading up to the house and mill Anne shared with

While everyone likes to call her the Julia Child of knitting, I prefer to think of Julia as the Elizabeth Zimmermann of food.

her partner, Marc Robertson. Most of us think of mills as being in old brick buildings along rivers, but once electricity replaced water power, mills could be anywhere you wanted. And in the 1980s, for boutique operations like theirs, it made perfect sense for Anne and Marc to put the mill in their own backyard.

The mill is just over the hill from where they used to raise a small flock of meat sheep. The flock basically paid for itself, but never more. Even meat sheep have to be shorn, so Anne did what many smaller farmers do: She paid the shearer in fiber, working the trade at about $0.50 per pound. One year, she changed her mind after shearing and asked the shearer if she could buy her wool back. Having already sold it, he put her in touch with the buyer, who happily offered to sell it back to her for $1.50 a pound. Something clicked. If that wool gained so much value in just those two steps, imagine what it could be worth as yarn?

They discovered that very few small-scale fiber processors existed, and those who did were extremely busy. It sounded like a solid business plan. Anne and Marc began investigating setting up a mill of their own.

Anne found a broker named Charlie Haynes. He'd worked in mills all his life and knew everybody. He took her around to see what equipment was available. Interestingly enough, nearly all the other prospective buyers she ran into on these trips were women. This was in the 1980s, when many American mills were upgrading their equipment, consolidating, or simply shutting down. In all three cases, perfectly good equipment was being sold for scrap. A new breed of small-scale custom operators stepped in, buying this equipment and launching mills of their own. This decade brought us Green Mountain Spinnery, Ohio Valley Natural Fibers, Frankenmuth, Yolo Wool Mill (now Valley Oaks), Brown Sheep Company, and Fingerlakes Woolen Mill (since closed)—and in February 1988, Anne and Marc joined their ranks, opening Blackberry Ridge Woolen Mill.

They began on a shoestring, buying salvaged machinery at junk prices from other mills to install in a building across the driveway from their house. They paid more for shipping than they did for any of the equipment. Bit by bit, the mill came together. They installed a Davis & Furber four-breaker woolen carding system like the one at Bartlett, the first two breakers dating from 1904 and the second two from 1905. Instead of a mule, they chose to go with its successor, a Whitin spinning frame built in Worcester, Massachusetts, in 1954. Anne still remembers the day an eighteen-wheeler arrived with a crane to deliver equipment. That same day, her neighbor decided to load up his tractor to move hay from his fields. It was possibly the only day in living history that her little country road had a real traffic jam.

The spinning frame was originally much longer, but Marc and another advisor, named Emory Benson, spent one spring sawing off the end of the frame and getting it working again. From the section they cut off, they salvaged as many parts as they could, stuffing them in their barn and attic in anticipation of future repairs. Thirty-plus years later, their stockpile of spare parts is running low.

"I saw one like this for sale a while ago," Anne said, shaking her head. "They wanted thirty-two thousand dollars."

Just out of curiosity, I asked her how much a new spinning frame like this cost.

"Oh I don't know," she said, as if I were asking her how much a solid gold car would cost. "Probably fifty thousand dollars?"

For all the tech startups that are praised for getting by on a $1.5 million "shoestring," I was astonished to hear just how low the entry point actually was for a small mill. Even if you added proportional costs for the carding machine, twister, cone winder, and skeiner, you could still get a brand-new mill up and running for less than the average cost of a house in the United States. Why on earth aren't more people doing this? And where is the venture capital to

"Oh I don't know," she said, as if I were asking her how much a solid gold car would cost.

help them? Are textiles such a dying industry? Or is it simply a matter of perception?

"You have to be a good mechanic," Anne explained. Early on she used to take things apart and clean them just to learn how they worked. Now she's developed more of an "if it ain't broke, don't fix it" attitude.

They were lucky to have Emory's help in those early years, since none of the equipment came with a manual. He had worked for decades at Portage Woolen Mill ("Ma went there!" chimed Meg), where much of their equipment came from. The next addition was a cone winder, built in 1939, followed by a small reeler (what we'd call a "skein winder") built by Johnson & Bassett in Worcester, Massachusetts, whose gold-flecked decorative laminate surface dates it to 1960.

After several years of managing to ply their yarn on the spinning frame—a feat of mechanical wizardry that involved getting the chain and gears to run backward—they finally splurged on an actual twister, also salvaged from Portage after they upgraded. Anne calls it the dumbest machine on the floor. The only thing you can adjust on it is speed. Run it fast for lace; slow it down for bulky. Any time one strand of yarn breaks anywhere along the line, you have to stop the whole machine. But it works.

Anne and Meg hadn't seen each other in years, so we stood in the shop at the front of the mill making small talk. Now only open by request, the space was full of Blackberry Ridge yarn that Anne sells online and at festivals. Behind it sat her office, and just off that, the mill. Anne finally gave us a "shall we?" and led us through a little door into the mill. Like a skilled landscape architect, Anne had placed the equipment such that it created its own rooms within the space.

Once she was sure we were standing out of harm's way, she started up the card, enormous and completely unprotected and as loud as a freight train. We all stood back in wonder. Wool fibers flowed like water through a complex series of different-sized cylinders. I lost track of Meg, who kept sneaking off to take pictures with the large digital camera she usually reserved for capturing the birds at her feeder or her two stunning cats, Bill and Ted. Liesl and her daughters kept a respectable distance, studying everything politely with their hands behind their backs. Every once in a while Meg would reappear and they'd chuckle about something.

I came in on the tail end of a story Meg was telling the girls about Oma and Gaffer, their nicknames for Elizabeth and Arnold. Apparently Oma once came home with forty skeins of yarn that had been on closeout at a store, and Gaffer had yelled, "You'll never use it all!" Of course she showed him, not only using it all but launching a yarn empire of her own.

Depending on where I looked, there was a feeling of either overcapacity or smallness. Each machine had its quirks—parts that have stopped working or never worked in the first place. Even with a sawed-off end, the spinning frame still dominated the space. Half of the twister and cone winder didn't work now, the parts having been scavenged to keep the other sides running. Yet the mill is always busy, with a backlog that keeps customers waiting for months at a time.

If any part of their much-coddled vintage equipment dares break, it can take months to find (or have made) a replacement part. When they had to redo the smooth cylinder at the end of the card (called a "finishing dopper"), the whole thing was out of commission for six months. The companies they rely on for parts change hands or go out of business. The last time they reordered more of the industrial-sized rubber bands that drive the twister tubes, they discovered that the company had been bought and now only makes the bands at a lighter weight that doesn't have enough strength. Anne asks them to recoat the bands, but . . . "We'll see when we reorder."

The mill is staffed primarily by Anne and her part-time assistant, Beth, who also works as a water-supply specialist for the state of Wisconsin. When not spinning yarn, she administers three parts of the Safe Water Drinking Act. Some days, they're also joined by Missy, Beth's gentle beast of an Australian shepherd. While Marc is still somewhat involved in the mill, he's ready to stop. It's a problem, Anne said, because she'd like to keep doing this forever.

"But if we have one thrown back," she confessed, "that's it."

On that first day, Anne called Marc in to run the picking machine so that she could continue the tour.

In terms of making yarn, the first few steps weren't too unlike what I'd seen at Bartlett. Fiber is received. If it's clean—and Anne really likes it when people deliver clean fiber—it goes straight to the picker. They have no duster. If it needs scouring, Anne does (somewhat reluctantly) offer this service in a back room. Instead of a scouring line like the one at Bollman, Anne has just two large washing machines to do the task, and stacks of mesh shelves for drying the clean fibers. This would not scale. Her scouring costs ten times what Bollman charges and takes weeks instead of hours—but it's the only option for those who can't meet the one-thousand-pound minimum at Bollman or Chargeurs. Also, for what it's worth, her scouring is impeccable.

While sorting through the wool I'd sent, Anne had already created a discard pile. (I told you she was exacting.) Apparently a few pounds had signs of water damage. The fibers had clumped together and were a slight orange-brown color. "I suppose I could've left a bit more in there," she apologized, "but it's better to be safe. You don't want that in your yarn." This explained the stain I'd seen in the bale, and the slight musty smell I'd noticed while we were packing it up. Please let this be the only wool in my bale that had been damaged.

Marc came in and donned a big pair of yellow protective ear-muffs, started up the picker, and began plopping my wool onto the spiked conveyor belt leading into the machine. The fibers would go through here twice, each time being blown into a little room.

The picker does such a good job of teasing open the fibers that they at least double in volume between the first and second run. On that second journey through the picker, the fibers are sprayed with a fine mist of high-grade spinning oil to lubricate them and tame any static, as was done at Bartlett.

"It's called Heather Lube," Anne explained. "It used to be called Topps Oil. It's a good emulsifier, and it washes out." She told me they don't use organic or natural oils, such as olive oil, because they tend to go rancid very quickly. Everything is a trade-off.

When they'd run all the fiber through the picker that second time, Anne opened the door to the little room. It was full of wool. The lower the humidity, the more wool sticks to the walls. The higher the humidity, the more you have on the (scrupulously clean) floor.

Soon Liesl took her daughters outside. Meg and I helped Anne gather the fibers and carry them over to a big bin (called the "feeder" bin) at the very end of the carding machine. Here another conveyor belt lined with metal teeth—this one running vertically—lifts fiber up and into a weighed bucket. By weighing the fiber before releasing it into the card, they can control the exact amount of fiber being fed into the card at any given time. This matters because what comes off the card is essentially yarn minus the twist. The more uniform the fibers are in thickness, the better. This explained what she'd done with my sample when she'd added weights to the feeder bin. Thinking the load weighed the full amount, when in fact it didn't, it dropped less fiber and produced a thinner web.

I could see that the first few teeth that the fibers went through were the hardest, strongest ones. They're the front line for the equipment, Anne explained—the checkpoint that filters out any oddities that may have found their way into the fiber. This can be anything from metal bale clips to hoof trimmings. They'd even found little toys once, probably left behind by children playing near the shearing area. Feathers, too, have a peculiar way of appearing at the most improbable moment.

The carding machine looked and operated exactly the same as at Bartlett. In the woolen-spinning world (both at Bartlett and here), yarn is really "made" on the cards. The spinning frame just adds a little stretch and twist to finish the deal. That said, the pencil roving coming off the cards will vary in thickness, depending on how thick you want your yarn to be. We were spinning a lighter-weight yarn this time, so the strands of pencil roving coming off the cards were correspondingly finer.

I should probably stop for a minute and talk about yarn weights. To those who don't use yarn, it can seem like a pretty standard material. But in actual fact, yarn holds the potential for endless variety, not just in color and texture and fiber content but also in thickness, or weight. A thicker yarn will produce a different-looking stitch than a lightweight one, just as a Magic Marker will draw a different line than a mechanical pencil. Everything we do with yarn is calibrated to its weight.

I decided not only to split my bale into four batches and have each spun at a different mill, but also to have each spun at a different weight—and to have each weight dictated by what that mill is best at doing. Some mills spin certain weights and fiber types better than others. As Eugene had said, if you don't know something, you hire people who do, and you learn from them. I'm letting the people operating the mill equipment—Lindsey, Anne, and whomever the final two end up being—decide what's best and teach me why.

Lindsey had spun a bulky-weight yarn to showcase the thick, oatmeal-like texture produced by his cards. Here at Blackberry Ridge, Anne's equipment is set up for shorter, finer fibers. Her cards could produce a finer, smoother strand of roving that could spin into a finer, smoother yarn. After running her tests with the fibers, Anne suggested we stay in the DK range (DK stands for "double knitting" and it refers to a lighter weight of yarn), and so that's what we did.

I still want to see what my wool would look like at a lace weight and in a heftier three-ply construction, but I'll have to wait and see what the next two mills say. For now, I'm loving how my first two yarns share a two-ply construction but are otherwise completely different.

Anne declared that the spool coming off the carder was full and shut off the motor. Suddenly we could all hear again. I watched Beth tidy up all the pencil roving ends and carefully tuck them into themselves like you'd twist a ponytail into a bun. She then hoisted the spool in her arms as if it weighed nothing and carried it over to the spinning frame, where she dropped it into a waiting cradle above a row of empty spindles.

Meg tapped me on the shoulder. "I think we're going to head out." I'd been so focused on the process that I'd forgotten she was still there. "I'd love to stay, but the girls have reached that point . . ." Her eyes gave a knowing twinkle. Earlier she had told me Cecilia was a budding ballerina. With Anne's help, we sent them away with a handful of my carded wool to stuff the toes of her pointe shoes. Meg had given her blessing to my bale, and I wanted to pass it on.

Hugs given at the car, I walked back inside just in time for a lesson on the spinning frame. While the mule spins a much airier and, in my mind, lovelier yarn, it makes yarn only half the time. The other half of the time, the carriage is busy winding the yarn onto the bobbins and making its return journey on the tracks. On a spinning frame, everything flows from top to bottom in one place. No need to pause and wait for the bobbins to wind up what's just been spun. It works twice as fast, and time is money. Especially in textiles.

Having placed the spool of roving on top, Beth began separating out each strand of roving and matching it up with the end of each pre-threaded spindle. She just rubbed the two ends together and presto, the magic of wool caused the fibers to adhere.

The spinning frame is ruled by two functions: draft and speed of twist. Both are controlled by giant, cartoon-like metal gears that can be swapped out, one for another, depending on what you need. Draft pertains to the amount of pull on the roving. The greater the draft, the thinner the roving becomes, but the easier it can break. Speed pertains to the rate at which twist is applied. Fine lace needs more twist than a thick bulky.

Everything on the machine is driven by gears, so we first made a best estimate of which gears would produce the yarn we wanted. Beth had to don rubber work gloves, as the gears are all covered in a thick layer of grease. Once the gears were set, Anne did a little last-minute oiling before turning on the frame and letting it run for a few minutes. Then we stopped, pulled out a sample of what had just been twisted, let it twist back on itself (mimicking plying), and weighed it on a McMorran Yarn Balance.

This handy device—once very popular among handspinners, then not offered at all, and now relaunched by someone else as a Yarn Balance—is just a clear plastic box that's weighted with sand at the bottom and has a little plastic teeter-totter balance up top. It is a remarkably accurate way to tell how many thousands of yards are in each pound of yarn—something mills like to use for guidance. You just cut a sample snippet and place it on a notch at the end of the teeter-totter arm. Then keep cutting and weighing it until it makes the teeter-totter sit perfectly horizontal. Then just measure the length of that snippet and multiply that number by one hundred. We were seeking a snippet that was an even twelve inches, which would represent twelve hundred yards per pound. The first few tries were far too dense and rope-like, so we kept shifting gears—literally—to increase the draft and reduce the twist. Eventually we had a light, airy yarn that balanced perfectly.

Beth kept scrupulous notes about each change in a spiral-bound notebook. A calculator was brought out. Numbers were thrown around. Both Beth's and Anne's scientific backgrounds were quite evident in their mutual passion for precision and their intolerance for fudging anything.

At last, we were ready to begin the production spinning. Anne turned on the frame and the spool of roving up top began to unwind, the ends running through a small silver "twister" tube that added a little twist but whose real role was simply to help the yarn move forward. The fiber then traveled between two rollers, the space between which is considered the drafting zone, before coming out the bottom, rotating on a flyer, and being wound onto a bobbin.

Behind it all sat a rotating felt-covered "scavenger" designed to take up the roving if something breaks or gets tangled. This lets all the other spools keep on spinning while the problem gets fixed. Both women kept an eagle eye on the bobbins. With each break, they snapped up the roving and pushed it onto the scavenger to collect while figuring out where the wool had problems. They know their machines so well that they tend to know exactly where the issues are.

It was fun to watch the two women work together, both being obviously so attuned to the equipment. Out of the blue Beth would say, "Did you hear that, Anne?" And Anne would answer with an "Mmm-hmm," shift her gaze to a spot on the floor, and then reach down to pick up some tiny piece of plastic I hadn't seen or heard drop.

That first day, we wouldn't get past spinning because of a crucial Blackberry Ridge rule: Always let the yarn rest overnight before plying. (Anne has many rules.) Wool, especially one with high-crimp fibers like my bale, benefits from resting after it's been twisted. I knew this as a hand spinner, but I doubted that the bigger mills could afford to pay it any attention.

Another Blackberry Ridge rule: Everything has to be run in forty-pound batches. Years of experience have taught them that forty pounds of fiber sits perfectly on the various-sized spools and bobbins required for each machine. Because there can be slight variances between each batch that runs through the card, they will never ply strands from the same batch together, either. They'll always wait

Wool, especially one with high-crimp fibers like my bale, benefits from resting after it's been twisted.

until they've completed multiple batches and then ply different ones together. It's another small detail that has the potential to make a big difference.

Lunchtime at Blackberry Ridge is an intimate affair. Because we were miles from town, Anne set out bread, cheese, cold cuts, and condiments on a folding table in her shop. Beth had made us a flourless chocolate cake for dessert, which we ate with the last of Anne's blackberries from the previous summer, freshly thawed and full of flavor.

It was such a distinct pleasure to sit with two smart, skilled women who knew how to make that entire mill go and who were more than happy to share their knowledge with me—without any bravado or awkward gender dynamics getting in the way. I knew that going forward I'd be working in very different mill environments. I savored my three days with them.

Only after a while did I figure out that Anne is not one for effusive praise. She is her own harshest critic, with incredibly high standards. She worked well with Beth, though. She gave her opinion whenever Beth asked a question, perhaps forceful at first, but when it came to fine tuning, she just stood, arms folded, smiling, looking down, saying, "You decide," or "It's up to you."

Having given our singles a good overnight rest, we could safely advance to plying the next day. But in order to do that, we first had to move the still-sleeping singles off the spinning-frame bobbins and onto the cones that fit on the twisting station. Every step in the process had its own particular bobbins (or spools, or cones, or spindles, or . . .). For this we used the half-functioning cone winder, whose non-functioning parts still jerked and wobbled in comical ways, like broken robots.

Then we took the cones to the maze of pegs set up on a frame above the twister.

Setup was no simple matter. They had to pair a cone from one batch with a cone from another, and then feed the end from each cone through its proper tensioning loop up high and then attach it to the flyer that circulates around the base of the bobbin. That's not all. Another of Anne's rules is that the cones all had to be carefully aligned so that both strands were fed into the twister *side by side* and not one on top of the other. Believe it or not, the position of those strands can affect the balance of your ply. As "dumb" as Anne claimed the machine was, it produced perfect results.

It took another day to finish twisting the singles into plied yarn. Meanwhile, Anne kept the spinning frame chugging away in the background until the last of our singles had been spun. The plump bobbins of plied yarn were given another overnight nap before they could advance to the reeler for the final step: Winding the yarn into skeins. Calculators and notepads were brought out for more testing, more weighing, and more math. We had to make sure they used the proper number of rotations on the reeler to produce a skein that weighed exactly four ounces. (Like Bartlett, Blackberry Ridge also prefers the Imperial system.) This proved to be the biggest logjam in the entire process. With the reeler capable of winding only ten skeins at a time, it would take Beth days to finish winding my five hundred skeins.

Another Blackberry Ridge rule: Skeins can never have more than one knot. Because of the capacity of each bobbin and the size of my skeins, this meant a one-in-seven chance of finding a single knot in any of my skeins. Knots are the bane of every knitter's existence, interrupting the flow of stitches and introducing a vulnerability to the fabric. Inevitably you have to unravel your work to the last row and re-start with the new skein. If your skein has two knots, or three, or four, this quickly becomes a major pain.

Most bigger mills have replaced knots altogether with a modern contraption called an air splicer, which does a passable job of making you think you have no knots in your yarn but still leaves a lump where one strand was blown open and wrapped around the other. I'd like to say that they've introduced this technology to keep their hand-knitting customers happy, but it all boils down to workload. Tying knots is tedious, and time is money.

I watched Beth patiently snip and tie every single skein before pulling them off the reeler, tying them together with twine, and depositing them in a large clear plastic bag that had been placed inside a garbage can. For all Anne's frugality—and she is one of the most frugal people I've ever met—these bags are a splurge. Orders will go out in recycled boxes from the grocery store, but each customer gets brand-new bags for their yarn. "It's 2 mil," she said. (That's two-thousandths of an inch; I had to look it up.) "It's not a wimpy bag." How like her to know the exact thickness of her plastic bags, which were, in fact, quite substantial.

Gorgeous as the yarn was, it was still weighed down with spinning oil that gave it a flat, almost cottony feel. Anne wouldn't even let me take any skeins home with me until she'd brought them into the scouring room, washed them herself, and set them out to dry. I could tell that she was even having trouble letting them go before they'd dried completely. "Be sure to set them out again as soon as you get back to your hotel room," she said as I was leaving. She would scour the rest of the yarn herself.

Already, the difference between unwashed and washed skeins was extraordinary. You almost couldn't tell that they were the same yarn—and you certainly would have no idea that they came from the same fibers as the previous one. What had spun up like oatmeal last time now carried the smooth refinement of jasmine rice.

Was the difference just because one yarn had been made on a mule and the other on a spinning frame? To a point, yes. But the real difference turned out to be in the setting of the cards themselves. There's a thing called "clearance," and it refers to the amount of space between each cylinder. The fine metal teeth on the cylinders should never, ever touch when they pass one another—nor should they be too far apart. It all depends on the average length of fiber you tend to run through the machine. Anne demonstrated hers by taking a fine sheet of metal and sliding it between two of the cylinders. That was her ideal clearance. Other mills will have a different clearance depending on the fibers they run the most often. Asking a mill to adjust its clearance for your order would be tantamount to asking a restaurant to adjust the height of all its kitchen work surfaces to accommodate a visiting chef. (An absurd demand except, say, if that guest had been Julia Child.)

I was beginning to understand that there is no one-size-fits-all mill for processing wool, no clever set of KitchenAid attachments that let you perfectly spin anything you throw at it. Each mill has equipment that's calibrated to do one kind of yarn really well. Which means that, among the handful of mills left in this country, depending on what you need to do, your options will be very limited.

And then there's scale. If I wanted to launch a sweater company and source everything in the United States, as much as I'd love to work with Anne and her mill, it just wouldn't be able to scale. My run was a lot. Her ideal order size is just forty pounds, small enough that she can really give it the attention it deserves. Forty pounds of yarn wouldn't even get you a set of sample sweaters from a knitting

---

What had spun up like oatmeal last time now carried the smooth refinement of jasmine rice.

company. Would she ever scale higher, to, say, five hundred pounds? She shook her head. "That gets boring."

Anne had given me three days of unfettered access to the mill, slowing down every process and explaining its nuance as she went along. The reason she was able to do this is also the reason why she can't be part of the solution to the bigger wool problem in this country. But she can sure make yarn.

It was time to advance to the next level of commercial yarn-making. My wool was about to meet the worsted system inside a much, much bigger mill. The kind that could make yarn for that sweater company, and indeed had for many years. But first? I didn't want my yarn house to have entirely white walls. It was time to pull out a brush, fill up a bucket, and start painting.

CHAPTER 8

JOURNEY TO THE HEART OF THE MADDER

LONG BEFORE THE INVENTION of Kool-Aid or Rit Dye, we had plants. Lots and lots of plants, whose bark, branches, leaves, berries, blossoms, and roots—not to mention the bugs that feasted on them—provided a rainbow of color when properly coaxed. It's called natural dyeing, and we still do it today.

Some learned their skill from modern-day pied pipers such as the late Luisa Gelenter of La Lana Wools in Taos, New Mexico, or the photo-chemist and botanist Michel Garcia. Others come from cultures that have been competently and unselfconsciously carrying on the tradition for millennia, for whom natural dyeing isn't as much a textbook process as it is an ongoing part of life. Nothing is written down; it is simply known.

Kristine Vejar met these kinds of people when she traveled to the Great Rann of Kutch, a desert region in the northwest corner of India, to study during college. She returned to India on a Fulbright to learn everything she could from these nomadic people about how their culture intersected with their textile and natural dyeing traditions.

Once back in the United States, however, the lack of suitable graduate programs in textiles led Kristine down the business path. For several years she worked with a company that made high-end mattresses out of ecologically responsible materials. She learned about the business side of textiles, from sourcing to application to marketing with integrity. She and her partner, Adrienne Rodriguez, settled in Oakland, started saving to buy a house, and figured they had their path figured out.

Then, on a lark, she took a three-day dyeing workshop with Bay Area fiber artist Claudia Hoberg. It was an *aha* moment. Suddenly all the things Kristine had observed in India made sense, things that she'd only partially understood in her halting Gujarati or in others' English as a second language. Soon, another purpose called to that nest egg. What if she used it to start a business instead? She would specialize in naturally dyed yarns.

Kristine quit her job and leapt in headfirst, renting a roll-up garage space within a business incubator. She soon needed a second space with the incubator, this one for a storefront—and then a third, which she used for a classroom and more yarn production. At this point, she knew it was time to take the leap and move into a larger space that could hold all the branches of her business.

She signed the lease on a retail space she'd had her eye on for some time in Oakland. Its high ceiling and spacious back patio called to her, and it had enough room for classrooms and community events. An architect friend drew up detailed plans and helped her navigate a multitude of building codes. It took three rounds of signing off before the space was approved. Then came the challenge of finding a contractor. At first they wouldn't talk to Kristine. "They'd just ask, 'Where's the man?'" she told me. But Kristine is nothing if not persistent, and on November 10, 2010, A Verb for Keeping Warm opened its doors.

By the time my bale came along, Kristine was up to her eyeballs dyeing yarn for the shop, running the shop, and writing a book of her own. But when I asked if she'd ever consider taking on a commission project such as mine, she said yes. Providence had prevailed yet again.

Whatever mental image your mind may conjure when I say the words "yarn store," chances are it wouldn't begin to describe what Kristine and Adrienne have done with A Verb for Keeping Warm. The vaulted wood ceilings and abundant light make it feel more like an aviary for a very special breed of wool-loving bird, complete with one of the most thoughtfully assembled collections of yarn you'll find anywhere. Tall, open-faced wooden bins are bursting with color that radiates with the brilliance of a Chagall stained-glass window. In the middle of the room, round skirted tables display more skeins sorted by vendor or fiber or color theme. (Kristine carries yarns from other like-spirited companies, not all of whom are committed to natural dyeing.) Glass doors lead to a dye garden in the patio out back. It's a lot to take in, and most first-timers need a minute to gather their senses. You can only gaze in wonder.

When she first started out, Kristine dyed yarns that she was able to buy wholesale from distributors. But she had recently embarked upon her own yarn journey, sourcing organic Merino wool from Sally Fox, a legend in the naturally colored cotton world who was now raising sheep. The wool was shipped to Green Mountain Spinnery in Vermont for scouring and spinning, and then dyed in Kristine's Oakland studio. She was a few steps ahead of me on this adventure, and I looked forward to learning from her.

Once Anne and Beth back in Mount Horeb had finished the yarn and shipped it to Oakland, I flew out and we got down to business. The first order of the day was deciding about colors. (But only after racing to my favorite restaurant the previous day to enjoy a plate of tamales and a strawberry agua fresca in the sunshine, as summer— and decent Mexican food—still hadn't yet reached Maine.) While indigo is by far the most exciting thing to see anyone dye, I wanted this to be Kristine's decision, so I asked her to choose a color whose process was, for her, the most interesting and rewarding. One that she could easily demonstrate during my visit, and one that she'd be willing to replicate across hundreds of skeins.

She walked me past the baskets of reds and purples and yellows, away from the cochineal, logwood, and weld, and toward a wall of more muted terra-cotta pinks and browns. These had all been dyed with madder, she explained. Kristine is tall and graceful, with the kind of posture that gives regal overtones to everything she says.

I was surprised that so many shades had come from the same material. Some were deep pink, like old-fashioned roses. Others had a touch more orange, moving to the clay roof tile end of the spectrum. And yet others carried the shades of a peach, from dark to light. It all depends on the percentage of dyestuff you use, she explained, and also somewhat on the amount of time you let the yarn sit in the dye. A teaspoon of Hungarian paprika in your chicken recipe will be very different than a tablespoon, and the same principle applies here with color. Not all the yarn bases were 100 percent wool, which added to the nuance. Each fiber absorbs and reflects color differently. Some of her yarns had silk, others were pure wool, while others had a dusting of alpaca.

In response to my questions about madder, Kristine led me out back to the dye garden and pointed to a vigorous patch of green growing in a raised planter. This was madder, she explained. A vigorous grower with sticky leaves, it spreads like crazy via underground rhizomes from which the dye is extracted. Most natural dyes involve a pound-for-pound exchange of materials, meaning for every pound of yarn, we'd need a pound of madder root. I'd sent her a little over sixty pounds of yarn to dye, and that planter itself couldn't have weighed more than a hundred pounds—and that was with the soil. How, exactly, was this going to work? She smiled and took me back inside. We turned right and ducked through a curtained doorway behind the cash register. We were now in her personal sanctum: the dye studio.

We'd left the yarn aviary behind and were now in an artist's workspace. Everything—the walls, counters, sink, stove, even parts of the floor—had taken on a patina of splatters, splotches, and drizzles, as if Jackson Pollock's preferred canvas had been wool. Shelves held assorted sizes and shapes of jars—some plastic, some clear glass. They all had blue painter's tape with tidy handwriting identifying the contents.

A teaspoon of Hungarian paprika in your chicken recipe will be very different than a tablespoon, and the same principle applies here with color.

She reached for a jar filled with what looked like cinnamon. Its label said, "Madder." Lacking acres of her own land across multiple growing regions and a crew of farmers, Kristine relies on dried, powdered dyestuff extract for all of Verb's production dyeing.

"What's the madder, you?" I asked, pointing at the jar. "Sorry, you probably get that all the time," I said.

"Actually, no," she replied, somewhat surprised herself.

I don't give puns to total strangers: I'd known Kristine and Adrienne for several years. We'd bonded over having all three graduated from Mills College, a marvelous if somewhat underknown women's college in Oakland.

Out came the calculator as Kristine carefully weighed several skeins and calculated the average weight. It's easy to ensure consistent skein yardage, but with wool, getting consistent skein weights is nearly impossible. The material does not want to be controlled to that degree. Kristine figured out how many skeins could fit in one of her large stainless-steel dyepots (seven), and how much madder she would need to dye that collective quantity of yarn. She created a formula, double-checked her numbers, thought about it for a minute, and then nodded. This was good. She spooned powder into a little cup on the scale until it weighed just right. Then she put the powder in a glass measuring cup and dissolved it in hot water. This would go into the dyepot after she'd filled it with warm water.

At this point the dye bath looked a rather unappetizing shade of rusty brown reminiscent of what might come out of a clogged sink. Like glaze on clay, natural dyes require heat to do their thing. It's one reason why weighing and measuring are so important. You can't eyeball it, since what you initially see isn't what you're going to get. We wanted a little flicker of variegation in these skeins, so Kristine dangled just their ends in the water for a minute or so before completely submerging the rest. A simple trick with lovely results, she assured me.

As the water warmed up and Kristine began nudging the yarn around with a pair of long-handled tongs, a splash of reddish brown appeared at the bottom of the yarn. It looked like someone had spilled Bolognese sauce on half a plate of spaghetti. But as the water continued to heat and Kristine kept gently prodding the yarn, the more color emerged. It would sit here on the stove, vaguely simmering in a bath of 145–150°F (63–65°C) water, for an hour and a half. Multiply this pot of seven skeins by the 250 skeins I'd sent her, and it meant she had another thirty-five dyepots to go. At ninety minutes per pot, that's more than fifty hours to dye all the yarn. That doesn't even include the prep work they'd done to get the skeins ready to dye.

After this dyepot had reached the right color saturation, the pot would be removed from the stove and allowed to cool so as not to disturb the yarn with any temperature changes or agitation (which would lead to felting). Then the contents of the pot would be poured into a plastic bucket (the studio was stacked high with tall white buckets that had been recycled from a neighboring gelato business) and allowed to sit for a day or so.

"This could be an old wives' tale, but I've heard that it helps with fastness," Kristine said. "The yarn used in the Persian rugs you see in museums, the ones made hundreds of years ago, that still have the red color? Those yarns often sat in madder for a month at a time. In a dry shady spot."

We'd jumped ahead and started dyeing yarn that had already been prepped earlier in the week. But now, it was time to see how that was done. The process, called "mordanting," makes it possible for natural dye to fix to fiber in a permanent way. It's a crucial step that enables that chemical reaction to take place and for dye to attach to wool fibers through what's called the "ionic process."

"Well isn't *that* ionic!" I exclaimed.

Most natural dyers, including Kristine, use aluminum sulfate for mordant—better known as alum. Adrienne took over this part of the demonstration. She, too, is tall (or maybe I'm just short?) with a straw fedora and the open, cheerful demeanor of a puppy. She brought out her own calculator, produced another notepad, and wrote a new list of numbers in tiny and precise handwriting. We had to figure out how many skeins would fit in each of these larger pots, and how much that amount of yarn would weigh. To that pot we'd add 12 percent of that yarn's total weight in alum.

"Why not add more?" I asked. "The *mordant* merrier, am I right?"

More gloves, more water, more spooning onto a scale, more stirring.

These pots sat on large burners in the patio out back, where Adrienne could keep a close eye on them to make sure the water got hot but never simmered. Every twenty minutes, she returned with a wooden stick to give the pot a stir. The yarn itself was in large lingerie bags to prevent tangling. When done, the exhausted mordant would be poured down the drain, its pH having been tested and disposal approved of by the city.

In between stirrings, I took a peek around the rest of the dye garden. While it's undeniably an urban space, they still manage to make it feel like a refuge. The concrete patio doesn't have nearly enough space to grow production quantities of anything, but it does offer enough room to grow plants for teaching and demonstration purposes—which they do, in pots and seedling trays tucked on shelves everywhere. Everything is carefully labeled with the name of the plant and the date it was planted.

The garden is more Adrienne's territory. She has ongoing experiments tucked on shelves, tall mason jars of sinister-looking liquids that looked like biological specimens. Things with mushrooms, walnuts, and eucalyptus bark, things that required weeks, sometimes months—and, in the case of the walnuts, years—to age. She tends to them every day, turning and shaking and rotating and feeding as necessary, always taking copious notes. You could say this is the Verb R&D lab. Production anything can lose its pizazz after a while. Being able to experiment keeps it fun.

"How'd you like to play with real madder?" Kristine asked.

"Ooh, yeah!" Adrienne perked up and ran off to find a hand fork.

She returned and loosened the soil at the base of one of the madder plants. I saw roots right below the surface, like buried electrical wires. She retrieved one vigorous clump and explained that ideally we wanted the root to be the diameter of a pencil, which would give us a better concentration of color. Root chosen, she pulled it loose from the rest, shook off the dirt, and gave it a rinse.

Like fresh turmeric, madder root starts to dye the minute you scrape its surface. Kristine donned rubber gloves and then, with garden pruners, she clipped the roots into little Chiclets-sized nubbins that she slipped into a women's nylon knee-high stocking. That would serve as a sort of teabag for the dyestuff. (While paper would be a far more eco-friendly solution, Kristine doesn't like that paper absorbs the dye. Nylon won't.) There couldn't have been more than a cup of madder root in there.

"Boy, we're really getting to the *heart of the madder* now," I said. Their laughs told me this might be my last pun of the day.

She tied the stocking with a knot and dropped it into a smaller pot of water along with a skein of undyed yarn. She brought it to a light simmer on another outdoor burner, where it would sit for an hour and a half. Every once in a while she'd lift the lid and nudge the yarn around. Gradually, a bright orange-pink-brown began to settle

In the natural dye world, indigo is the ultimate hat trick. It's magic.

around, and eventually on, the yarn. It was far brighter than what we'd seen indoors, a more vivid and tropical sort of peach color.

I was still marveling at the madder when Kristine's foot kicked a gelato bucket and she had another idea. "How about indigo?" she said. "Would you like to play with that?"

In the natural dye world, indigo is the ultimate hat trick. It's magic. And if anyone offers you a turn at an indigo vat, especially if it's a perfectly composed one, as I knew Kristine's would be, you do not even pause before saying yes.

The indigo process requires a book all its own, but in very simple terms it works as follows. Leaves from the *indigofera tinctoria* plant are harvested and carefully composted before being fermented in water and wood ash. The process takes time and results in a liquid that has been depleted of all oxygen. You know you've done it right if a copper-colored scum begins to grow on the surface and the liquid looks green, not blue. Now, all you do is drop yarn (or fabric, or whatever) into the liquid and swirl it around until you're satisfied. The yarn will look green at this stage. But pull it out of the vat and give it a squeeze. Immediately the liquid begins to oxidize, transforming that green and everything it's touched—don't look away or you'll miss it—into blue.

With so much time and energy and materials required, it's no wonder that natural dyeing fell out of fashion the minute we figured out a cheaper, faster, and more consistent and stable way to dye with chemicals. But you have to admit, there's something deeply satisfying about plunking roots and yarn in a vat and ending up with a beautiful color. It has a primal feel to it, like cooking over an open flame, or, come to think of it, knitting your own clothing. You're looking at the same colors that were in use five thousand years ago.

I willingly sacrificed one of my skeins for the vat. I dunked, swirled, waited, and then slowly pulled out my skein. It was a gorgeous sort of tropical light green you'd expect someone from Tampa to wear. I squeezed out the liquid, dangled it in the air, and—like donning a mood ring and waiting to see what it had to say—I watched in wonder as a delicate sky blue washed across the fibers. It's a birth and baptism. Fibers that began as one color, then turned another color in the vat, now transform, upon taking their first breaths, into something else entirely.

If I couldn't take home the madder-dyed skeins, could I at least take this yarn home with me? If I promised to hang it out and let it dry overnight? "No, Clara." Kristine gave a disapproving shake of the head, and I knew that, after having already exhausted her with puns, I'd tumbled even lower in her esteem. She went on to explain that indigo requires yet more steps to ensure that the color fixes to the fiber. And after that, it'll still rub off on your fingers or needles or any other surface—a process called "crocking"—while the color molecules work their way into the fiber. It can take months of wear before finally settling down.

So no, I couldn't *indi*-go home with my skein. (That was a bonus just for you.) In fact, I wouldn't see it again for weeks.

Speaking of settling down, I wondered if Kristine and Adrienne had ever managed to replace that nest egg and buy a house. She shook her head. They're still renting. And the soaring housing costs in the Bay Area were making it increasingly difficult to staff the store. Kristine didn't say it, but I wondered if those same costs would eventually cast a shadow over their own future in the Bay Area, and that of their colorful oasis. I hoped not.

CHAPTER 9
RUST BELT REVIVAL

IT'S A MUGGY MORNING in late May. The bale has taken me to Nazareth, Pennsylvania, a sleepy hamlet of 5,600 located two hours and fifty years away from New York City. It once supported three union-backed cement plants and a raceway frequented by local legend Mario Andretti and his family. Its Main Street is a time capsule to lost prosperity. The old hardware store hangs on, as does the Army & Navy Store, the barbershop, and the corner grocer with its illuminated Hershey's Ice Cream sign and American flag that waves in the breeze. There are a lot of American flags in Nazareth.

The architecture here is an exquisite mix of late-eighteenth and early-nineteenth-century Revival and late Victorian, with even older stone buildings dating back to before the Moravian Church relinquished civil control of the town in 1858. Proud brick homes have graceful wraparound porches and freshly mowed lawns with generations-old rose bushes. The Nazareth Historic District, starting at Center and Main Streets, was added to the National Register of Historic Places in 1988.

Occupying more than three acres along south Main Street is an older mill complex. The paint on the wooden window frames is peeling, and at least one tree is sprouting from between the bricks. In faded paint beneath what was once a water tower for the oldest building is the name Kraemer Textiles. I'm here to meet a family that has been spinning yarn for generations, and to watch my third yarn be spun. Theirs is one of few American textiles manufacturing dynasties still surviving, albeit much diminished and in a castle that's no longer theirs.

Kraemer Textiles was already a successful hosiery manufacturer when the Schmidt family bought it in 1907. That year's *Davison Blue Book Textile Directory* noted that it employed 280 people, offered finishing and dyeing services, and had 113 knitting, 100 ribbing, 45 looping, and 7 sewing machines in operation. Later, when political unrest in the Pacific Rim threatened their silk supply, the family responded by converting the business into a spinning mill. Not too long after that, Kraemer Textiles became one of the first mills in the country to spin synthetic fibers.

By the 1980s, business was booming. They were spinning 300,000 pounds of yarn per week, much of it destined for the carpet industry, but some for garments. On any given day, their yarns were in three, four, or more pages of the L.L.Bean catalog. Had my imaginary sweater business existed in the '80s, this would have been my mill. Business was so good, they bought their competitor and swelled to five hundred employees.

Just a few weeks after that fateful acquisition, DuPont announced it was moving away from Orlon, which had been Kraemer's bread-and-butter fiber. Over the next year, Kraemer lost millions of dollars in revenue. Then NAFTA was enacted, and orders dried up as companies shifted production abroad. More and more customers and suppliers closed their doors as the industry continued to decline. Kraemer ultimately whittled staff down to forty. They sold off all their buildings and a good deal of their equipment, doing everything they could to stay afloat.

It's the same American story you hear over and over again, one of tragedy and (hopefully) resilience, with generations of family lore relegated to a framed photograph in a grandson's bedroom. But the company *did* survive. Far leaner and more efficient, but still intact. Today, Kraemer spins an average of thirty thousand pounds of yarn per week. Small in comparison to the 1980s numbers, yes, but still significant. If you set out all the yarn Kraemer spins in a week, it would still circle the globe three times.

If you set out all the yarn Kraemer spins in a week, it would still circle the globe three times.

Two brothers now work for the business, David (President) and Victor Schmidt (Corporate Secretary). A sister rents an office upstairs for her graphic design company. The whole building is rented from new owners, the brothers having sold it years ago. "We did what we had to do," David told me more than once, "to still be here."

David is the Senior to David the Junior, his son, who works with him downstairs in the mill and goes by Dave at work to avoid confusion. At one point two other Davids worked for them, and the joke was, "If you can't remember someone's name around here, just call them David and there's a sixty percent chance you'll be right."

I'm here not only because of the mill's compelling history but because it is one of the only worsted mills left that can still comb fibers. Most others buy combed top directly from Chargeurs in South Carolina, or send their wool to Chargeurs to be carded first. (I'd been told that their minimum was one thousand pounds and that they wouldn't comb fibers that had been scoured elsewhere, so Chargeurs had been out of the running for this project.)

My first two bale yarns had been spun woolen. Now I wanted to see if my wool could spin up into the kind of smooth, worsted-spun yarn that all the hand-dyers were using. They always relied on a dusting of silk to make their colors pop, so I needed someone who had access to silk and could add it to the mix. Kraemer checked all the boxes and was happy to take the job.

David had originally gone to college to study music. His passion was piano. But the more he heard other people play—brilliant newcomers like Chick Corea—the more he questioned his skill. Perhaps sensing his doubts, David's father asked if he wanted to come home and work at the mill instead. He said yes, and he's been here ever since. David oversees everything that's produced at the mill. As soon as his son Dave was out of diapers, he'd made the mill his home, too.

"I was driving forklifts by the time I was twelve," Dave told me. He went to college on a full scholarship as an environmental sciences major but quickly grew disillusioned with the outdated facts that the professor was teaching. He left and eventually joined his father at the mill. He also works as a volunteer firefighter. While machining a part in the Kraemer machine shop (that, too, was sold), he lost two-thirds of his middle finger. I was warned to watch for a wiggle in the remaining digit when he's particularly angry about something. He'd been lucky. A friend lost his entire arm in a carding machine. Seeing my grimace, he added, "They're so slow to shut off, they keep rotating even after the power goes."

Working upstairs as far from the actual mill as you can get without leaving the building is Victor, the younger brother. Victor manages all the staff and administrative operations from a dark, wood-paneled office I'm guessing belonged to his father, and his grandfather before that. It was filled with file cabinets. In the adjacent office, I met a woman who had come to work for the company when Victor was ten. "He used to sharpen all my pencils," she said, shaking her head with a smile. "He'd hand me back erasers."

The building's main entrance opens into a bright, spacious yarn shop that was a gift from David and Victor's grandfather to his wife, an avid knitter. To your left, the administrative offices, Victor's realm. To your right, at the opposite end of the store, is a door leading to a large windowed room they call "the lab." This is the Davids' domain, and it houses a small-scale card, pin drafter, and spinning frame they use to work up production samples for customers.

Open shelves hold years of yarn samples that they've spun for people. A sink, microwave, and jars of dye help customers envision the finished product, although Kraemer no longer offers dye services. Their proximity to the legendary Philadelphia dyer G. J. Littlewood

Canisters are the clue as to what kind of mill you're in. If you see a tall canister with swirls of soft-serve fiber in it, you're looking at a worsted or semiworsted mill.

& Sons puts them at a geographic advantage over the few other remaining mills in this country.

In the far corner of the lab, a staircase leads down into a catacomb of basement corridors. When navigated correctly, you end up in a massive mill space that begins in the rear of the building and then continues—through a jagged hole that looks like they just hit it with a wrecking ball and went about their business—into a vast cinder-block building. There was no insulation, no air-conditioning, and the midday heat was overwhelming. But it was impossible to tear myself away from these machines. I was spellbound watching them work, watching people manipulate the gears, feed fibers through rollers and onto conveyor belts, move tall canisters of fiber from one station to the next.

David led me to the cards, which looked nothing like the massive circus calliope of cylinders I'd seen at Bartlett and Blackberry Ridge. All I could see here was a huge green metal box that looked more like a transformer at a power station than any sort of textiles gadget. The only clue that this had anything to do with yarn was the conveyor belt of fibers marching into the machine and several streams of fibers squirting out nearby, like a woolly soft-serve ice cream dispenser. Each stream dropped into a separate canister, the carded fiber looping around and around, layer upon layer, until each canister was full to overflowing.

Canisters are the clue as to what kind of mill you're in. If you see a tall canister with swirls of soft-serve fiber in it, you're looking at a worsted or semiworsted mill. If you see the long spool with individual strips of roving, like we did at Bartlett and Blackberry Ridge, you're looking at a woolen setup. Kraemer had several cards busily chugging away on a huge lot of green fiber when I arrived. Some canisters were already topped off with fiber and looked like key lime soft-serve cones that had begun to melt.

From the cards, the canisters are dragged to the machines that are most crucial to worsted spinning: the pin drafters and combs. Think of wool like hair. The woolen system works best with short curly hair, as in the fine crimpy wools shorter than three inches (7.5 cm). You give it a few quick passes with a soft bristle brush before gathering it all into a fluffy, jumbled ponytail of yarn. The worsted system, on the other hand, needs longer hair, or wools longer than three inches (7.5 cm). You still give it a good brushing, but then you go back over it with a comb and slowly work every fiber into submission. If spinning systems had personalities, I like to compare the two to Gilda Radner (woolen) and Jane Curtin (worsted).

The Warner & Swasey Servo pin drafter is actually part of a three-step system the Davids call "the finishers." The mission here is to make the fibers as parallel and uniform as possible by pulling them through a series of metal pins and an auto-leveler that mechanically adjusts thick and thin areas. They'll run fibers from multiple canisters together to further blend and unify what comes out the other end. While the woolen system used a good amount of oil to help the fibers hold together, here they only needed a little bit of oil to lubricate the fibers and control static. Once run through the finishers, the resulting fiber is called "sliver," pronounced "sly-ver."

Most of what Kraemer spins has already been combed into top and needs only one pass through the finishers. But if you were to present them with a wool they'd never used before, as I was, they'd have to run it through the combs, too. "Otherwise, it's a horrible yarn," said Dave.

Some other mills still have pin drafters, but Kraemer is, to my knowledge, the last commercial-scale contract mill in the United

States with its own combs. These amplify the tidying and aligning of the finishers, with actual metal "combs" that rake through sections of sliver at lightning speed and remove short, neppy, and irregular bits.

The combing machine, a beautiful Schlumberger imported from France in 1988, is Dave's domain. He proudly demonstrated it to me, explaining the mechanisms, removing the protective cover, and cranking the combs and brushes by hand so I could get a clearer, slower look. He told me you can still buy new combing machines, but he prefers these older ones. They have more gears and settings he can hack to do whatever he wants. The new ones are far more specialized and consequently can do fewer things, making them harder to tweak.

"Of course there's an art and a science to all of this," Dave said. "Some settings can do two things on different days."

All I knew was that I was losing a lot of fiber in the combing process—nearly half of what I'd sent in. Not only is time money in textiles, but so is *wool*. That's the other reason I had them add silk to the mix: to make up for some of that fiber loss. I was secretly worried there wouldn't be enough yarn for all of my Explorers. And wouldn't that be unfortunate.

The spinning portion of operations looked nearly identical to what I'd seen at Blackberry Ridge, only on a bigger scale. We passed three massive green spinning frames that stood proud but empty, patiently waiting for their next job. "These came from Ireland," David said, running his hand along the metal casing. "My grandfather custom-ordered them from Mackie in the 1960s. They broke the mold after they made these." He gave the machine an affectionate pat.

In the 1960s, Mackie, which began as a manufacturer of flax-processing machinery before shifting to military production during both wars, would have just begun making its synthetic spinning equipment. Brand-new, these would have been as state-of-the-art as you could get. "We had eight," David added. They had to sell off the other five.

Farther on we reached more spinning frames, these made by Saco-Lowell and sporting 240 bobbins on each side. The bobbins were perfectly spaced in a line that appeared to stretch forever, like the Rockettes in formation, preparing to kick. Despite less equipment, it was still easy to imagine how this place cranked out what it did in the 1980s.

The spinning frames were fed by hundreds of slivers running through a maze of PVC pipes overhead and to their respective canisters on the other side of the walkway. Once on the frame, the sliver is pulled through two draft roller sections before it receives twist that's been formed by a traveler sliding around the base of the bobbin at thousands of revolutions per minute.

Walking past a massive cone-winding setup, David stopped to introduce me to a woman tending the machines. "She's worked here for thirty years," he said. She smiled. "Her sister and mother worked here. Her father did, too." Quietly to me he added, "He just died." He gave her a pat on the back and we kept going.

On my second day, Victor intercepted me at the door. "How's it going down there?" he asked. "Is it going okay?" He'd been eager to show me the town that was so important to his family, and I was eager to hear his story, so off we went. We left his aging, chocolate-brown cocker spaniel, Mocha, curled up asleep on a chair in his office, one of the only rooms in the mill with any form of air-conditioning. It wasn't even 9 a.m. and the late-May heat was already oppressive.

He drove me around what used to be the entire mill property. "That place now stores cardboard boxes," he said as he pointed to one building. "That's rented by people who make bathing suits, I think," pointing to another. Bit by bit, like an English estate after the war, everything had been sold.

Just that morning I'd passed a funeral home bearing their family name. "Yeah, if you go back." He waved his hand. "I forget how we're related." We passed an ominous building in the architectural style of an 1800s orphanage that turned out to have been exactly that, also run by a distant relative. Nearing an intersection, he pointed out a building that used to be a bank and was owned by another Kraemer. "I have a dollar bill with his signature on it!"

Yesterday David told me that even when he was in college studying music, he knew he wanted to come back and work at the mill. I was curious if Victor felt the same.

"Oh no!" he said. "I never, *ever* wanted to work for the mill." He'd studied primary school education in college but quit after just a few weeks of practice teaching. He then went to restaurant and hospitality management school, eventually landing a job managing a chain of restaurants. He loved the work, but the pay was abysmal. This was the 1980s, when business was booming back at the mill.

One day his father said, "Why don't you come on home?"

He decided to give it a try, "much to my brother's . . ." His voice trailed off. "My brother and I are very different."

We continued driving uphill, winding through wooded neighborhoods he'd apparently never seen. "Oh, this is pretty," he said, glancing at a park.

"Didn't you grow up here?" I asked.

"Sure, but I haven't lived here in a long time," he answered. He lives in Bethlehem, four miles away.

We detoured to see the Martin Guitar world headquarters, perhaps the only international corporation still based in Nazareth. Once made by hand, the guitars are now manufactured on an assembly line.

From there, we drove back into town, stopping at the small brick building that was the first Martin Guitar headquarters. Now its downstairs houses the Chamber of Commerce. Correction: *one* of Nazareth's chambers of commerce. Apparently this town has two dueling chambers of commerce, a spin-off having been formed after this, the original one, had done such a disappointing job of saving Main Street.

"They've been looking for you!" Eleanor exclaimed when we returned. Eleanor is the mother figure of the group, an intermediary between upstairs and downstairs, brother and brother. Her husband wants her to retire, and the Schmidts desperately want her to stay. She works in the yarn side of the business as a gifted knitter, designer, and teacher. "I love being here," she said.

David did a good job of concealing any annoyance at my having been kidnapped for the morning. "We have yarn for you!" he said with a smile, handing me two white skeins.

Now is as good a time as any to come clean: Kraemer was spinning two yarns for me. When I bought the bale and wrote my wool mentor Elsa for advice, she casually mentioned that she, too, had an extra bale that was more than she needed. Two bales, in fact, of exquisite Cormo wool from a ranch in Montana. Emboldened by the positive public response to my bale project and flush with a little leftover cash from my crowdfunded "student loan," I told Elsa yes before I'd even learned how to make yarn out of Eugene's bale. Now Kraemer was spinning two yarns for me: one with Eugene's Merino, the other with Elsa's Cormo. Not too long after Elsa, a British farmer made me another offer I couldn't refuse, and within a few months I was the proud owner of a literal *ton* of wool. It's a slippery slope, my friends, this yarn making.

At any rate, they'd just opened my Cormo bale, run it through an opener similar to what the previous two mills had, and carded the fibers. They ran them through the finishers in the hopes that we'd have a good enough yarn not to need combing, since I was wary after losing so much wool in the bale yarn. For this one, they'd spun four plies and twisted them together into the skein David was proudly holding.

But the fibers I'd bought turned out to be a bit shorter and finer than their equipment liked to handle. "Maybe it's lamb's wool?" David offered. I'd never even thought to ask Elsa and wouldn't have understood the consequences even if she *had* said it was lamb's wool. But apparently I'd gotten the somewhat shorter end of the sheep.

They'd been hoping to be able to spin it right then, but the fiber would indeed need to be combed. The sample yarn was shaggy and irregular. I gave David the bad news. He nodded, probably knowing I'd say so, and down we went, back into the bright open mill. We found Dave and gave him our report. He nodded to another man standing nearby, and together they began dragging the canisters over to the combing machine.

As we walked back upstairs, David asked, "I hope you like Indian food?" Nazareth was full of surprises. The previous day, Victor had brought us sandwiches from a Wawa convenience store. We all ate together around a long table in the yarn shop upstairs. For dessert, we each got a cookie in its own paper sleeve. It was like elementary school, only there was no place to take a nap.

Today, at that same table, we feasted on some of the best take-out Indian food I'd ever had. We continued the conversation from where we'd left off the day before, talking more about the family business and yarn, about how their grandfather had built the yarn store as a gift to their grandmother, and how Eleanor was soon heading to Africa with a church group. Knowing their story, how important this business was to the family and how hard they'd worked to keep it going, I felt almost embarrassed by their generosity. I should have been the one bringing *them* lunch.

Dave had returned upstairs and was about to fill up his plate when his father interrupted. "As long as there's yarn to be spun, you shouldn't be up here eating." He nodded, put his plate back, and returned downstairs. Yesterday, he'd missed his kids' first trip to the zoo. Today, he'd end up eating a pint of strawberries while working through lunch.

Later in the day, Victor informed me that he'd planned a little gathering on my behalf. How'd I like to join him, Eleanor, and two other knitters for dinner? David and Victor rarely socialize outside of work, Eleanor later explained, but she'd insisted Victor invite both

Davids, "so that they would have an *opportunity* to say no." (Which they did.) And so a few hours later, Eleanor pulled up at my hotel in her much-loved Honda Odyssey, with the odometer reading 228,429 miles, and we made our way to Bethlehem.

Our first stop was Victor's condo, located in a renovated steel mill. It had thick brick walls and tall factory windows that faced directly onto a bridge. The traffic was just feet away and going so fast, one wrong turn and a truck would land in his living room. "Sometimes I forget it's there," Victor said, pointing to the traffic, "like when I'm getting dressed in the morning."

He showed me that framed dollar bill he'd told me about, the one signed by his relative. It was hanging slightly crooked in the entryway among other, also slightly crooked shadow boxes of family mementos. On another wall, this one in his bedroom, he pointed to an elegant framed lithograph of the mill complex during its heyday. It, too, hung slightly askew. I didn't know Victor well enough to feel comfortable giving the frames a nudge, though it was hard not to.

Back in the living room, he pointed out a shapely wood-and-steel coffee table made by a local artisan who takes old I-beams from the Bethlehem Steel buildings and incorporates them into furniture. All around were relics of industry past. His pride of place, and connection to it, was abundantly evident. Before dinner, he gave us a driving tour of Bethlehem, slowing so we could admire the handsome old brick buildings and picturesque downtown with a bookstore purporting to be the oldest in the country.

At the restaurant we were joined by Clara, who works at the mill and dreams of hiking every mile of the Appalachian Trail, and by a friendly woman from New York who loved France "but not the French" and insisted that all vegetables be removed from her plate. The women were clearly used to dining out with Victor, and they bantered back and forth in a familial way.

I was charmed by how much these women loved knitting. I mean *loved* it, as in they would happily do it all day, every day, if they could.

Their enthusiasm was uplifting. I didn't have the heart to tell them I spend more time testing and writing about yarn these days than I do knitting anything for fun. I wanted them to believe that their dream really was possible. (And maybe it was?) When Clara asked, "Tell me, what do you do when you aren't knitting?" I was grateful for the distraction.

Meanwhile Victor filled us in on what was happening in Bethlehem since the Bethlehem Steel Plant shut down in 2003. It had been turned into an arts and entertainment district with a television studio, a casino, and the ArtsQuest Center. They'd kept the foundry's five massive blast furnaces and were using them as a backdrop for a performance venue (fittingly called the Levitt Pavilion SteelStacks), of which Victor is a proud board member.

Over dessert, Victor rolled up his sleeve and showed us a line of stitches.

"Do you think this is healing right?" he asked.

They all leaned in and gave it a good study and took turns reassuring him. He turned to me with a smile and whispered, "They're like my mothers."

All at once I could see the little boy who'd charmed the office staff into letting him sharpen all their pencils down to nubbins. And I could see why he came back to the area and to the mill.

It seemed like a Tennessee Williams play, these two very different brothers held fast by the invisible tendrils of family honor and obligation. If history and globalization had their way, their business would not exist. Yet it does, running smarter and faster on vapors of what it once was, with a skeleton crew and a fraction of the original equipment. It's the twenty-first-century industrial version of selling the silver, firing the butler, moving into the gardener's cottage, and doing their best to preserve the heart of their family's legacy. In other words, adapting.

Kraemer Textiles' main work continues to be synthetic blends for industrial applications—things like ropes, rugs, and buffing pads.

Customers look to them to produce yarn they can proudly market with a "Made in America" label.

But the company has found an unexpected niche in the handknitting yarn market, both in the yarn it sells under its own label and the yarns it makes for others. It is also uniquely positioned to spin sufficient quantities of yarn for that mythical American sweater company, should one ever arise.

Customers look to them to produce yarn they can proudly market with a "Made in America" label. Hand-dyers are seeking domestic mills from which to source their un-dyed materials, and knitters are increasingly compelled to track down domestically produced yarn. It's become an important business for them. In any given year, nearly half the hand-dyers exhibiting at the national needle arts trade show are Kraemer customers. They've found a sweet spot that would've made their knitting grandmother very proud. It may not carry the mill, but it'll definitely help keep the lights on.

CHAPTER 10
TREE HOUSE CONFESSIONS

TO WALK THROUGH the steps a commercial yarn company would take when making yarn in this country, I'd need to reckon with the runaway phenomenon that is hand-dyeing. In the yarn world of late, hand-dyers have taken on a cult status. Head to a festival and you'll see people lining up, often hours ahead of time, to be among the first at that year's darling dyer's booth. They'll sprint through the fairgrounds like shoppers the morning after Thanksgiving, picking the shelves clean before anyone else has managed to get in.

You don't even need to leave your house anymore to partake. You can stay at home in your pajamas, refreshing your browser again and again until the designated hour, minute, and second when a tiny amount of some new special hand-dyed yarn goes up for sale. In one collective gulp, every last skein is swallowed whole in a feeding frenzy that is both mighty and terrifying. The victorious crow their success. The thwarted walk away disheartened, discouraged, and more determined than ever to nail that next release.

For my Master's of Yarn-Making curriculum to cover all the bases, it was time to take my yarn to a hand-dyer and watch her (or him, only in this case, her) ply her trade. I wanted to see what kind of person becomes a hand-dyer, and what this person's daily reality looks like. But there was a problem.

Most hand-dyers use the same basic yarn: a multiple-ply, worsted-spun, machine-washable Merino, sometimes with a touch of nylon, or silk, or cashmere. Kraemer was well versed in spinning these kinds of yarns for hand-dyers. I even had them add a dusting of silk to my yarn to ensure that the colors would really pop. (I'd also lost so much wool during combing that I risked not having enough yarn to go around. The extra silk was the metaphorical iceberg lettuce to make my burrito bigger.)

But my wool had ended up being too short and fine to spin into the stereotypical hand-dyer's yarn. It was looser spun, far more delicate, and with a hint of unpredictability. It hadn't been run through the chlorine-polymer shrink-resist system at Chargeurs. It was not, by any stretch, machine washable.

I needed a dyer who had experience working with fibers that weren't machine washable. Someone who was comfortable with that hint of unpredictability, who could do this in a timely manner and not turn the whole run into one giant felted mess. Someone who was willing to reveal her process to me.

If you thought Apple was tight-lipped about its development process, try approaching a hand-dyer about her process. In a market where everyone's using the same handful of yarn bases from an even smaller handful of mills, and dyeing them often with the very same dyes, nothing distinguishes one from another except for individual color aesthetic and process.

I immediately thought of my friend Jennifer Heverly, the same Jennifer who'd played Thelma to my Louise in Texas. Early in the life of her business, Spirit Trail Fiberworks, she'd obtained rare and unusual wools, made yarn from them, and hand-dyed it. She could deal with the unpredictable. She also knew how to coax emotion and nuance out of silk blends, which had increasingly become her

I'd also lost so much wool during combing that I risked not having enough yarn to go around. The extra silk was the metaphorical iceberg lettuce to make my burrito bigger.

preferred base. She was also the very best kind of perfectionist, with organizational skills that made me look like a squirrel. I knew she'd do a good job in a timely manner. And because we were friends, I might even be able to convince her to pull back that curtain a tiny bit and reveal some of her process to me.

Jen's story parallels that of many hand-dyers who turned to a creative field after bottoming out in corporate America. She'd spent more than a decade at a high-powered job managing commercial real estate in Washington, D.C. At one point she'd had twenty people reporting to her. She was on the fast track, but she was losing her life in the process.

She and her husband, Brett, moved to the country and built their dream home on land her parents had bought in Rappahannock County, Virginia, where she'd spent her summers as a child. While it's distinctly rural, its proximity to Washington, D.C. (just ninety minutes in good traffic), has made it a weekend hamlet for the Beltway crowd. She's just down the road from the Michelin three-starred Inn at Little Washington.

Jen's architect father designed the house, and they built it using almost exclusively wood harvested from the lot. Nearly every piece of wood is local, from the exterior to the stairs, floors, bookshelves, kitchen cabinets, and even the countertops. So, too, were the woodshed and nearby tree house for the kids.

Signs of Jen's creativity are everywhere in her house. She and her family made the stove backsplash tiles themselves, covering them with handprints and abstract doodles and scratchings. A stained-glass window (also made by Jen) illuminates the high peak above the front door. On the walls, her framed paintings and drawings sit among mounted deer heads from Brett's hunting expeditions. "I drew the line at four," she said. "I told him if he wanted any more, he'd have to build a man cave."

A windowed stairwell dominates a large open space that combines the living room, dining area, and kitchen. Two bare, angular tree trunks run up the center of the stairwell from basement to attic, giving one the feeling of being in a tree house.

Jen runs her dye empire from a computer at the kitchen counter where she can preside over the goings-on of her two teenagers, Jackson and Caragh, and whichever friends might be visiting at the time. Kids are always coming over. "I'm the cool mom," she likes to say.

Her actual dye studio is downstairs, with sliding glass doors looking out onto a covered patio where the dyepots reside. That's a somewhat Photoshopped story. The truth is that this popular hand-dyer did all her work, thousands of skeins a year, out of a walk-in laundry closet off her family room. The sliding glass doors lead to that covered patio, pots, and burners.

"People keep writing and asking if they can come visit my studio, as if I actually have one," she said. "I can't show them this." She pointed to the large cardboard boxes stacked in corners around the TV, couches, and treadmill. She had even more stored in the trailer she takes with her to shows. Another corner had several wooden drying racks laden with freshly dyed yarn from the day before, a fan blowing to circulate the air. "The yarn does make a good humidifier in the winter," she admitted.

For years, a studio was an ongoing bone of contention in her household. Her father had drawn up plans for something so much smaller than what she'd specified, it sparked years of debate about the value of her work and its legitimate need for a proper space versus what other people thought she needed. After my visit, she would finally move her operations out of the house and into a spacious, formal studio. But for more than a decade, this was it. A domestic situation mirrored by many other extremely popular and prolific hand-dyers.

Like the majority of her peers, Jen uses synthetic dyes. They operate on a much simpler, less idiosyncratic basis than natural dyeing. Mix powdered dye with water, splash it on your yarn, give it a cook, and you're done. I oversimplify, but not by much.

But even using this easier route, the yarn has to be prepared first. Instead of calling it a mordant, Jen uses the term "acid assist." This makes the fiber more receptive to dye; it can be something as simple as vinegar. Jen prefers a one-to-one ratio of citric acid and vinegar, but don't tell anyone.

Today we'd be dyeing three batches of the bale yarn spun by Kraemer. Each would contain two bundles of five skeins—so thirty skeins. She'd already given the yarns an acid assist. She'd also dyed me three possible colors (on her own yarn) to choose from. We didn't lose any skeins to trial and error, which was good because I had no skeins to spare. She knew the dye recipe and could repeat it consistently.

I'd asked Kraemer to skein the yarn and ship it directly to Jen, which they did. The cardboard box had self-destructed in transit, arriving partially taped back together and with several skeins sticking out, their frayed fibers covered with a greasy black smudge.

This was my first time studying the yarn up close, and my heart sank immediately. I knew it would be dramatically different from the first two yarns. But it was nothing like the springy, tightly spun yarns that hand-dyers use, which had been my entire goal. Instead, it had two very loosely spun, loosely plied strands that looked like they'd fall apart at any minute.

My mind flashed back to the last day of my Kraemer visit. It had been unbelievably hot in the mill. I'd been sweating in places I didn't even know I could sweat. I'd rejected their first sample as far too loose. I'd watched Dave don the giant rubber gloves and tinker with the greasy gears at the end of the spinning frame.

When he brought me the second sample, it still wasn't perfect. But it was better. I was starting to feel guilty about taking up so much of their time for so tiny a project. I was also worrying about how much wool I had left, and how much wool each test had used up. I talked myself into believing the yarn would be fine, and I told him to proceed. Any disappointment in this yarn was entirely my fault.

Jen had been wary of me photographing and documenting too much of her process because it was, to her, what made her work unique. As soon as I saw her process, I understood why.

A little background first. Most hand-dyers will do some form of immersion dye, where you plunk a skein into a pot of dye and let it work its magic. Or you plunk part of the skein into one pot, and then plunk the other side into another pot. Or you drizzle another color in halfway. Something. It always involves a big pot filled with dye.

But Jen used no giant dyepot whatsoever. Instead, she spread out the skeins to be dyed on a table covered with plastic. She added varying quantities of five different dyes into three huge canning jars, topped them off with water, and then donned a pair of yellow kitchen gloves as if she were getting ready to scrub the tub.

She picked up the first jar and sloshed some dye onto the recumbent skeins. She set down the jar and began to massage the dye into the yarn. Not a light tap, either, but with a pressure and ferocity of a masseuse at a Turkish bath. It looked like she was squeezing, but she said no, she was using her upper body to push the dye into the yarn.

As soon as she was satisfied with one area of yarn, she'd pick up the jar and slosh dye elsewhere. Then came more pushing, pushing, and pushing, this time as if she were wrestling dough into submission. I could see a faint glisten of sweat build on her forehead and upper lip. This was intensely physical work.

On a busy day, Jen dyes forty to fifty skeins, which is a lot of pushing. A few years ago she began having back problems that almost put her out of commission. After realizing that her dye table might be at fault and putting it on riser blocks, the pain went away.

It was hard to believe that the yarn could absorb those three jars of color, but it did. When she was done giving them their spa treatment, she lifted the skeins. Not a single drop of dye remained on the table.

Satisfied with her work, Jen gave the yarn a light spritz with another acid assist, rolled up each five-skein bundle in plastic, and

In variegated yarn, you want the dye to hit, or "strike," the fibers instantly, which happens with heat. If you don't, the colors will migrate as the water heats up.

took the bundles outside to one of the waiting pots. They'd been used so much over the years, they'd developed a patina of copper and gun-metal gray.

She'd already put water in the pot and lit the burner so that everything would be hot the minute those skeins hit the steamer tray. In variegated yarn, you want the dye to hit, or "strike," the fibers instantly, which happens with heat. If you don't, the colors will migrate as the water heats up. And, as we know, Jen doesn't like it when colors have a mind of their own. She closed the lid and left them to steam for about ninety minutes to make sure the heat hit the very centers of the skeins. They never touched boiling water. It was the steam heat that set the color.

While we waited, we got to talking. I asked Jen how she came to this technique, which was so different from anything I'd seen before.

"Oh, easy," she said with a laugh. "I'm a control freak."

With immersion dyeing, you can't control where, exactly, the color goes on the skein. You just drop the whole thing into the pot, kerplunk, end of story. Jen prefers to physically apply color to each inch of yarn, directing each splosh and press until she likes what she sees. Sure, during steaming the colors can still move around a bit until they settle on receptive fiber. That's how her skeins can look identical going in and still come out with variegation. But she still has far more control over the finished product. And control is something she likes.

Jen began her business in the early 2000s. She'd given up a stressful office job to stay home, take care of the kids, and help with the back-office part of her husband's landscaping business. But that wasn't enough. She grew passionate about rare sheep breeds and about dyeing yarn, and soon realized she could easily start a business at home. It would give her the freedom to take care of the household while also doing something creatively fulfilling for herself.

This was long before Ravelry and Etsy, when just a smattering of hand-dyers existed on any national scale. Thanks to her husband's business, she hadn't felt tremendous pressure to have this support the family immediately. "I started small, doing what I could manage," she told me. "The more routine it got, the more productive I became."

By the time I arrived with my yarn, Jen had two assistants helping several days a week with yarn preparation, finishing, and packing. She dyes yarn five days a week, about forty weeks a year. She now has more than five hundred repeating colorways, and even more one-of-a-kind colors. "In the thousands, I'm sure."

When she's preparing for a big show, she'll dye eighty skeins a day, flat out, until right before the event. "But that's usually because I should've started dyeing for the show in early July and didn't start until the end of August." Her mother occasionally helps, although she's been relieved of yarn-labeling duties after her particular form of cursive turned the color "Caledonian Pines" into "Caledonian Penis." (Those labels are now a collector's item.)

As the buzz has grown about her business, as more people sprint to her booth at shows to snatch up the latest colors, Jen has found herself at a turning point. If this were purely about business, the next logical step would be to hire people to help her dye. That would allow her to take on more wholesale accounts and release more yarn throughout the year.

"But I don't want to do that," she said. "People who buy my yarn know who dyed it—that I personally touched the yarn. I think that's an important part of what I'm selling." Even if it ultimately limits her growth, she's fine with that.

Dyeing is what she loves most. She told me the story of her father, an accomplished artist who got a job as a draftsman at an architecture firm. He did so well that he kept getting promoted until he eventually became a partner in the firm—by which time he'd lost all opportunities to draw. She doesn't want to repeat that mistake.

Jen also benefits from having spent twelve years in commercial real estate. It wasn't all that fun when she was doing it, but now she can appreciate the business lessons she learned, things like negotiating with vendors and managing staff and cash flow.

She notes that things are easier today than they were early on. "People are no longer scared off by things they've never heard of before. They're more willing to take risks on hand-painted yarn made in small batches by a stranger," she said. "They're more educated and accepting of small dyers."

When asked what advice she would give newcomers, Jen immediately answered, "Don't quit your day job."

Social media can make this look like a dream life with huge profits. But the truth is that, even now, she can't support her whole family on this business. Few do.

"No matter how much you love doing something," she continued, "there are going to be days when you hate it. But you can't stay in your pajamas and watch movies and eat bonbons."

She admitted that she sometimes looks at her friends who stayed in real estate, at their plump 401(k)s and their nannies and their tropical vacations, and she wonders if she made the right choice. But at this point, after more than a decade of total creative freedom, she knows she could never go back to the corporate world again. She chose freedom and flexibility, at whatever cost. "This much I know," she said. "I could never take direction from anyone else again." She'd never admit it, but I suspect even my dye commission was a bit of a push.

When the yarn had been fully steamed, Jen turned off the gas and let the skeins cool overnight until they were back to room

What had been loose and puffy and delicate was now the texture of crushed velvet. The color was a flickering grayish blue and turquoise, like peacock feathers.

temperature. She then filled her trusty washing machine with water and a dollop of Synthrapol, a fabric detergent that's really good at removing excess dye that might cause the colors to bleed later. She gently dropped in the skeins and let them soak for forty-five minutes. (I should note that at no point did she actually set the washing machine on agitate. Her machine will spin a load dry without shooting more water on the fibers, which could cause them to felt.) She spun out the water and rinsed the skeins one more time in warm water to remove the Synthrapol. Finally, she draped the skeins on one of the wooden clothes racks and let them dry overnight.

Bright and early on my last morning, two assistants arrived to help prep the skeins. Wool yarn tends to get shorter when you use heat and moisture to dye it, because the heat and moisture reactivate the fiber's innate crimp and springiness. Hang an un-dyed skein and a dyed skein side by side and chances are the dyed skein will be visibly shorter.

Jen doesn't like how blotchy her yarn can look when it comes out of the steamer, so she takes the added step of re-skeining the yarn at a slightly larger circumference so that the colors are more randomly distributed. I know of no large-scale operation that would go to this trouble, but the results were worth it. Now that I could see the finished yarn, I was struck by how much it had transformed.

What had been loose and puffy and delicate was now the texture of crushed velvet. The color was a flickering grayish blue and turquoise, like peacock feathers. I'd seen a lot of yarn, but never anything quite like this. My yarn failure now made me look like a genius.

One by one, Jen's crew picked up a skein and held it taut between their upright hands as if they were playing cat's cradle. They'd give it a good shake. And then, in one seamless motion, they'd rotate one wrist a few times, lift the skein up to their chest, tuck their chin down right in the middle of it, bring the ends together, and then lift their chin just as the two sides of the skein twisted back together again, like a perfectly formed pastry. It was a beautiful, well-practiced action that took longer for me to write than it did for them to do. Each skein was carefully stacked inside a plastic bag until all had been twisted. This was only part of the batch. It would be several more days before Jen had completed the whole lot.

So far, this hands-on process worked for Jen. And in general, it serves the craft industry remarkably well. The colors were gorgeous, and her technique had rendered an already unusual yarn even more unique. She has no interest in taking on staff and churning out thousands of skeins every month, so scalability really isn't a concern. With pricing at current levels, she doesn't need to scale. While many knitters still balk at paying more than $6 for a pattern, they're increasingly comfortable spending upwards of $25 for a single skein of hand-dyed yarn if it's billed as small-batch and in some way artisanal. In fact, the going rate for a rather basic machine-washable Merino yarn base, if dyed by the right person, is now in the mid-$30s.

What works well for individuals is proving fatal for larger yarn companies whose reputations have been built on offering a broad, unvarying selection. For those who want to stay alive and capitalize on this trend, their only option is to partner with a hand-dyer. Finding one who'd be willing to dye their yarns consistently, in the volumes they need, at a rate far lower than retail, and on tight deadline, is nearly impossible.

If we bring this back to my bigger goal of that imaginary American-made sweater business, there's no way this could ever scale. Besides price, commercial knitting and weaving industries require far more yarn and it must be on cones. I doubt any of them would return an email if you proposed sending them a handful of 100-gram skeins. No matter how pretty the color.

Who could dye my yarn in those quantities? At a price that wouldn't make my sweaters the exclusive domain of the 1 percent? A commercial dyehouse, that's who. I had one batch of wool left from my bale, just enough to spin a final yarn befitting of a dyehouse.

First I needed the yarn. And that, my friends, was proving to be a challenge.

CHAPTER 11
SAVED BY THE BALL

MY SELF-IMPOSED Master's of Yarn-Making program had covered a lot of territory. Thanks to Eugene, I'd attended a shearing and seen the inside of a commercial scouring plant. I'd successfully managed to get my bale fibers onto the last commercially operating spinning mule in the United States. I'd learned how the mule works, and I'd seen how its successor—the spinning frame—did somewhat similar work in a far speedier timeframe. I'd observed my little batch of fibers run through capital-b Big mill equipment, the kind that used to supply multiple pages of the L.L.Bean catalog. And I'd witnessed the natural dyeing and synthetic dyeing processes up close with hand-dyeing masters.

But these people and places had generously opened up their worlds to me, sometimes letting me hopscotch in front of bigger, legitimate customers, because they knew me. With the exception of Bollman, which was entirely Eugene's doing, all of these businesses had deep ties in the handknitting world. They knew my work; they understood the opportunity in this project. They were willing to inconvenience themselves a bit, knowing the cause was good. They had shown me the steps required for a yarn company to manufacture wool yarn in the United States, except for one key factor: I wasn't a yarn company. I was a familiar face pretending to be a yarn company.

My bale's last yarn would be the final exam. I needed to approach an even bigger mill with as little handknitting awareness as possible. No upstairs yarn shop, no house line of yarn or sweaters, no beloved Eleanor swatching away and giving feedback. I had already been slowly advancing up the food chain, from mills that spun just a few hundred pounds a week to ones that could produce thousands of pounds a week. This last mill needed to be even bigger, the kind that really could supply my imaginary sweater business and then some. If my fibers were too short for the worsted system, I would go back to woolen for my final experiment.

I knew of a mill in Massachusetts that could do the job. It had no website, no catalog of house yarns to choose from. I only knew about it through my friend Pam Allen, who'd overheard a conversation about it at the mill where her yarn was made. Her mill had fallen behind and subcontracted some of its carding to this other mill. That second place—called S&D Spinning Mill—processes between 1 million and 1.2 million pounds of wool every year. The people at S&D had no idea who I was, and they had no particular interest in taking on my work. Pam would make introductions, but I'd have to seal the deal. The training wheels were officially off.

We began with a nervous, hurried conversation that wasn't encouraging. They asked me to send fiber samples to be sure they could spin them. I waited weeks until finally mustering the courage to call them back. (I may have mentioned already that I'm extremely phone phobic?) They'd lost my number, they claimed. We had a more friendly and encouraging follow-up conversation this time. Yes, I could visit the mill. They'd be happy to show me around. But they could make no guarantees about when they'd be able to spin my yarn. That was in August.

Since Pam had introduced me to S&D, it seemed only fair to include her in this final mill trip. Pam was a touchstone of the knitting world. She was the original author of *Knitting for Dummies*, then editor of *Interweave Knits* magazine, and then creative director at Classic Elite Yarns before launching her own startup, Quince & Co. Since S&D had begun spinning yarn for her as well, she was eager to tag along, and I knew that two brains and two sets of ears would be far better than one.

The drive from Portland, Maine, to Millbury, Massachusetts, is about 140 miles. In good traffic, that's only two-and-a-half hours. But it's longer if your passenger assumed you knew the way, and you assumed your passenger knew the way, and you eventually had to pull over and put the address in your respective phones. We were given competing directions at twenty-second intervals all the way from Worcester to Millbury. After passing several abandoned mill buildings along a winding river on the outskirts of town, we found our way to S&D.

In 1753, a man named John Singletary built a mill here. The imposing four-story brick building was positioned at the edge of a man-made pond fed by a small stream fed by a lake. The water from the pond ran under the mill, activating turbines that, in turn, ran the equipment. It was such a source of pride for Millbury that the building was used on the town seal.

By the late 1950s, the mill had been abandoned, the building left empty and in decay. That's when Frederick Dearnley entered the picture. He'd worked his way up to be superintendent at another mill when the owner suddenly died. The widow who inherited the mill had no real interest in running it, so she and Dearnley worked out a creative financing arrangement. She became a silent partner (she was the "S" to Dearnley's "D") in a new company, S&D Spinning Mill. It began in the town of Grafton in 1957 and moved to the Millbury building in 1961. Eventually Dearnley bought out his partner but kept the name.

Frederick's son had taken over by the 1980s and was running the mill with the help of his five sons: David, John, Jeffrey, Tom, and Scott. Times were good. The spinning order for just one L.L.Bean sweater—the Kingfield—represented about 150,000 pounds of yarn per year.

After NAFTA, things started to dry up. Businesses shifted manufacturing operations to cheaper places like China, India, and

Between 2000 and 2011, seventeen U.S.
manufacturers closed every single day, and
the worst hit were in textiles.

Mexico. L.L.Bean moved production of its Kingfield sweater (among others) overseas, and not only did S&D lose the work, but Pine State Knitwear, the South Carolina company that had manufactured those sweaters, soon went out of business.

Between 2000 and 2011, seventeen U.S. manufacturers closed every single day, and the worst hit were in textiles. At the same time our friends at Kraemer were busy selling off property and laying off staff to stay afloat, the brothers at S&D were similarly applying every ounce of New England resourcefulness to survive. But eventually they had to face facts. One left to take a job at AstraZeneca. Another bought a house in Florida and made plans to move, while a third put his house on the market. The American Textile History Museum in Lowell had come and chosen the equipment they'd be able to save. (Ironically, the museum itself would close a few years later.)

In 2007 a miracle happened. After several years of submitting test batches, S&D secured a contract that would bring the mill back to capacity. They would pick, card, and spin the yarn that wraps around the rubber core of every Major League baseball.

Today, operations are divided among two buildings: the original brick mill and a newer cinder-block structure where the twisting, packing, and warehousing take place. Between the two buildings is that stream-fed pond that originally powered the mill turbine. The turbine is also still there, but it's too far gone to be put back in use. And because the mill was built around the turbine, there's no way to replace it without dismantling the building. So there it sits.

We were greeted by Jeffrey, the middle brother. He was tall and slender, looked to be in his late fifties, with silver hair, thick glasses, and a sincere smile. He wore a green, short-sleeved work shirt that was tucked into matching green work pants—standard wear for the men at the mill, I'd soon discover. He told us he spends his day running between buildings, doing a bit of everything. His older brother John runs the spinning side of the operations, and John's son now works at the mill, too. "His daughter worked at the mill for one summer before she came to her senses," Jeffrey said with a wink.

John was away on vacation that week. He'd set everything up to run in his absence, but they'd just discovered that the fiber they'd been sent for the current baseball run was "having problems." Their contract stipulates that the blend of fibers in the yarn must be 85 percent wool, with no more than a 3 percent variance. They don't actually control what fiber they receive from the supplier, and this morning they learned that there was too much wool in the mix. They had to finish carding what they had on the machines and then wait.

While Jeffrey walked us across the yard to the mill building, he began telling us his story. I was immediately struck by an uncanny coincidence. Remember Victor Schmidt at Kraemer? The brother who never wanted to work for the family business and instead got his degree in hotel management, only to be eventually drawn back into the mill? Well, Jeffrey had never aspired to work at the mill, either. He got a degree in hotel restaurant management. He had worked as a purchasing agent for a hotel in western Massachusetts and lived in California briefly.

"I loved it," he said, "but they didn't want to pay me anything."

Eventually he came back to the mill, just part-time at first to help with the cone-winding, but in the end he was back full-time. Just then, we passed the old time clock in the brick mill building, each employee's card carefully tucked in its slot.

When they're ready to run a batch of fiber, Jeffrey explained, they move it across the yard to the mill and hoist it up to the top floor with a rope and pulley system. Many early mills used a gravity system in their manufacturing process, lifting heavy materials to the top floor and then letting gravity carry them from floor to floor through chutes and ducts until finished product emerged at the bottom. Bartlett ran this way, too. Here on the top floor, the bales were opened, their contents spread out and run through a picker. Sometimes the baseball bales were so tightly packed that they had to hack at them with axes to loosen them up.

The floor was still littered with remnants from the recent baseball run. It looked like a stuffed animal factory had exploded: There were tufts and bits of all sorts of unidentifiable material everywhere.

Nearby, a younger man (also in a green work uniform) was replacing a broken leather drive belt.

"Stuff is always breaking around here," said Jeffrey. "What's hard is when we have to manufacture the replacement parts." I thought about my grandma's Elna sewing machine languishing in the attic because of a broken belt that nobody makes anymore. Even the sewing machine repair guy urged me to take it to the dump, but I couldn't.

The inside of the mill building revealed its age, with low ceilings and crooked floors, everything having obviously been repaired multiple times, often with duct tape. "We go through a lot of that around here," Jeffrey confirmed.

On one wobbly wooden pillar hung a clock that played birdsongs every hour, not that you'd be able to hear anything when the equipment was running. A calendar was pinned on an adjacent pillar with a woman in a black bikini and high heels leaning against something I couldn't quite make out.

Jeffrey went on with the tour. After the bales are opened and the fiber is picked, it's blown through big tubes to a room downstairs, where it then gets fed into one of five Davis & Furber carding machines, all nearly identical to the one I'd seen at Blackberry Ridge. I'd never seen so many in one room, and the effect was stunning, like suddenly finding oneself in the midst of a marching band.

Davis & Furber had once been the largest manufacturer of its class in the country, building more woolen cards and spinning mules per year than any other manufacturer in the world. S&D was able to get replacement parts from them until as recently as 1981, when Davis & Furber finally closed, marking the demise of the last domestic supplier of carding equipment.

Each card was surrounded with sliding chain-link panels to keep things—like arms, or bodies—from being pulled in. It's a common mill nightmare. "The controls are at the far end of the card," said Jeffrey. "When things are running, you'd have to scream pretty loud to get anyone's attention."

We went down another floor and into a spinning wonderland. I counted six Davis & Furber spinning frames, each in perfect working order and all operating simultaneously. Now I was smack-dab in the middle of the brass section of the band, each frame blasting its note at full volume. The mechanics were nearly identical to Blackberry Ridge, except that the felt-covered "scavenger" roller had been replaced by tiny vacuum tubes behind each bobbin. If the yarn breaks, it automatically gets sucked into the tube. Snippets are collected and reused elsewhere. They were in the middle of a batch of fine, tight black wool. The customer name was written in chalk on the metal board at the end of each frame: "Navy." While the baseball work makes up about half of S&D's workload, another 20 percent is dedicated to commission spinning for the U.S. Navy.

Down another floor we went. I didn't realize how much grease was being used on all this equipment until I slipped in the freight elevator. "Careful," Jeffrey cautioned. "That grease gets carried in here on the bottom of people's shoes." If the metal floor was slick, I could imagine how saturated the wood floors were from centuries of use.

Once on the ground floor, the equipment got a little newer, the environment quieter. The most ingenious machine at the mill sits here—a high-tech cone winder that takes spun yarn off the spinning frame bobbins and winds it onto cones that then make the journey across the yard to the twisters. Kraemer had one like it, but it wasn't being used the day of my visit.

It takes several bobbins to fill a single cone, showcasing the ingenuity of this machine. Nobody needs to stand at attention, shutting everything off when one bobbin runs low, tying knots, and restarting. It all happens automatically by air splicing.

Multiple bobbins sit on a sort of rotating lazy Susan. A strand is drawn up from the first bobbin until it runs out—which the machine is cleverly able to detect. At that point, a little mechanical hand reaches down and grabs the loose end. The base rotates and pops the empty bobbin onto a conveyor tray that carries it to the end and plunks it into a waiting bin. Meanwhile, the base has advanced to the next bobbin. Another small mechanical hand reaches down and grabs the end from that bobbin—"grab" isn't quite the right word, as it uses suction. Finally, one yarn end is blown open and wrapped around the other, making a glorious "thwoooop" sound.

We wandered back out into the sunshine and toward the twisting building before Jeffrey remembered something he wanted to show us. "It's out here," he said, motioning us toward the busy road. Looking both ways, we ran out to the middle of the street. At our feet was a Millbury town sewer cap. On it, the town seal depicted the very same brick mill building we'd just left. He was cut short by Pam's yell of "Car!" and we ran back to the side of the road and toward the newer building.

Twisting at S&D is nearly identical to what happened at Bartlett, Blackberry Ridge, and Kraemer, but instead of twisting individual cones of singles together, S&D pairs however many strands that are to be plied together and winds them, side by side with no extra twist added, onto another bobbin. Then *that* bobbin is fed into a machine that applies the actual twist. All of this takes place on equipment that's varying shades of green metal and covered in the kinds of blinking buttons and knobs you'd expect in a 1950s science fiction movie.

Something had been nagging at me. How did they know exactly how much twist to apply to the yarn, either in spinning or plying? Jeffrey opened a metal cabinet and pulled out a chart.

All the magic numbers were here. What I found most fascinating (or disconcerting) was that the chart made no variation for fiber content. It's a well-known rule in hand-spinning that longer fibers don't need as many twists per inch as shorter ones. But this chart gave one number no matter what. If the singles had been given a certain number of twists per inch, regardless of the length or texture of the fiber, there was only one number for plying.

Jeffrey conceded that they could change the numbers depending on what the client wants. "If you want a soft yarn, we can do that," he said. The U.S. Navy, for example, required a super-strong yarn with ten twists per inch. He walked us over to a small batch of alpaca being twisted with far fewer twists per inch. I'd never thought of specifying yarn in terms of "hard" and "soft," but in a way, it made sense.

The oldest brother, David, came back from lunch. He, too, was tall and slender with silver hair, thick glasses, and a friendly face. And he, too, wore a green work uniform.

"So, what do you think?" he asked, beaming.

His brother's path had been so similar to that of Victor at Kraemer. I wondered if *this* David felt about the family business the way Kraemer's David did about his. Sure enough, he said he'd never wanted to work anywhere else. Even as a young boy, he loved working at the mill. He'd work eight full hours every Saturday, refilling bobbins for $1 an hour. He said that their father is now eighty-three but still brings the mail most days. If the mail includes a check, he makes them stop whatever they're doing and take it to the bank. "He has a fit if we keep him waiting even two or three minutes," David said. "He still comes first."

We walked past a loading dock full of boxes and into another cavernous space that's usually filled with fiber for the baseball run. Sometimes they get as many as seventy bales at once. Through another door was a smaller room where the other clients' fiber goes.

When I first spoke with John and tried to explain my yarn project, that I wanted to help promote his mill to other people who make yarn, he seemed dismissive. "We're almost at capacity," he'd said. "Any more business and we'd have a problem." Any *less* business and he'd have a problem, too, which is why this room exists. It's where they hedge their bets with smaller clients.

He walked us to a heap of boxes that belonged to an alpaca cooperative. Members from around the country bundle up their fleeces, one or two or ten at a time. They come in recycled boxes of all shapes and sizes, some with handwritten address labels, others listing a FedEx store as the shipper. When the pile gets high enough, they pop everything open and spin it into yarn.

Moving down the line, I spotted three bales wrapped in heavy-duty clear blue plastic, the product of our friends at Bollman. Just a little farther, I recognized my own bale bag expertly strapped to a wooden pallet and rather impatiently awaiting its turn on the equipment.

It was getting late. We'd stopped their work long enough, and we needed to hit the road if we wanted to avoid rush-hour traffic around Worcester and Boston. After we said our thank-yous, David ran back into his office and came out with a brand-new Major League baseball still shrink-wrapped in its plastic box. "Please," he said. "I'd like you to have this."

My heart felt an unexpected tug as we pulled away. I hadn't met any of these people until that morning. We'd only spoken by phone, and my initial impression hadn't been all that great. (It turns out whenever the office phone rings, a horrible siren blares throughout the building. Who wouldn't be a little grumpy?)

We'd arrived on a day when they were down one key person, another had just left for lunch, and their biggest job was having problems. You'd expect a little impatience, a surreptitious glance at the watch, even a sarcastic comment or two.

There was none of it, nor did any of them dumb down their language or use a patronizing tone. They welcomed us warmly, proudly showing us this place that's been a focal point for their family for three generations. They took time to explain everything, answer questions, and share their personal stories. Knowing the struggles they've faced was at once heartbreaking and inspiring.

The next Monday, I spoke with John. He apologized for missing my visit and for not having spun my yarn yet. His vacation reentry had already gotten off to a bad start.

"We're having electrical problems with one of the cards, and of course the electrician is on the Cape," he began. "But we'll try to run white by Friday, and when we do, you're the first in line."

But then his voice brightened. "So," he said, "how'd you like the mill?"

CHAPTER 12

HALLOWEEN SPOOKTACULAR AT THE HAUNTED DYEHOUSE

PROMISES, PROMISES.

It was actually two months before S&D would spin my yarn. Elsa had warned me that I'd need to be both patient and persistent on the journey. I was fine with the patience. I'm good at drifting down streams. The persistence part was much more difficult. It's not in my nature to be a squeaky wheel, to push back at someone else's time-frame, to pester.

But that's what it took to get the yarn out of S&D in time to meet the final deadline in my Master's of Yarn-Making program.

Having spun this yarn at the biggest mill yet, it made sense to dye it at the biggest dyehouse I could find. The kind you'd rely on if you were starting, say, an American yarn company. Or a sweater company, although mine was looking less likely by the minute.

My options were even slimmer than those for mills. I knew of only two commercial dyehouses that were suitable for a job of my size. Of those, I chose the most obvious option, a business that knew me and where the bale had begun its journey.

On Halloween, I loaded up the car one last time and headed south on the Maine Turnpike, exited onto Route 1, and followed it south through the town of Saco. I passed storefronts decked out with ghosts and goblins and pumpkins, my car went bumpety-bump over the train tracks on which the Downeaster Amtrak train travels on its way to Boston, and finally, after passing over the turbulent waters of the Saco River and into Biddeford, I turned right into the familiar parking lot of the Saco River Dyehouse.

This was it: the Great White Bale's last stop. A collision of delays and other commitments (not the least of which was a book launch and tour) had kept me from seeing the finished yarn until I arrived in Biddeford. I'd asked S&D to spin me a well-balanced three-ply yarn, that kind of Number 2 pencil yarn you could use for just about anything. They'd done a fine job, although I detected a hint of shagginess. I'd seen the rough baseball stuff that had gone through the cards, the sturdy wool they'd been spinning for the U.S. Navy, the long alpaca fibers. Those should've been my clue that the cards were calibrated for something not as short and delicate as Eugene's wool. Still, even in its flat and oil-laden state, the yarn was beautiful.

The realities of making any yarn in this country had worn me down. I was just glad it was done.

A few things had changed at the dyehouse since my explosive bale-opening escapade at the beginning of the year. A new brewery occupied the empty space we'd walked through to reach the back of the dyehouse. The Quince offices now had the look of a well-oiled fulfillment operation. And the dyehouse had expanded to fill nearly every available square inch of space. A work schedule that was once relatively open was now filled with jobs as more yarn companies heard about what was happening in Biddeford. Not content to dye just wool and other protein fibers, Claudia was working to bring in package dyeing operations that would open them up to the synthetic realm.

When I'd first toured the place in January, right after the dyehouse had started up, it was still under the direction of Don Morton. A master of color on fiber, Don had been in charge when the dyehouse was in Massachusetts. There he helped produce a full spectrum of colors for yarn companies such as Reynolds, Jo Sharp,

---

The realities of making any yarn in this country had worn me down. I was just glad it was done.

and Paternayan. Don had wanted to retire. But when that dyehouse folded and Claudia, Pam, and two others teamed up to buy the assets, he'd agreed to come along for the transition. By April, Don had left and Muhammad Malik had taken over as dye-master.

Claudia made introductions and then left us to get on with our work. Malik, as he likes to be called, hails from Lahore, Pakistan. He comes from a family of chemists. He has his master's in chemistry, and his sister, father, and father-in-law all work as chemists. It may therefore not come as much of a surprise when I tell you that his wife, Raana Jabeen, is also a chemist and has worked as his assistant for years.

With diligence and luck, Malik worked his way up the textiles ladder from lab worker to lab manager, then supervisor, then mill manager, and eventually general manager with the multinational Indus Group. In that capacity, he was responsible for the dismantling of cotton mills in South Carolina, North Carolina, and Alabama, as Indus moved operations overseas. Over the course of three years, his team filled 358 containers with the guts of these mills, shipped them to Pakistan, reassembled them, and brought the equipment back to capacity. So high was Malik on the corporate ladder that during his last five years in Pakistan he didn't even have to open his own car door—someone else did it for him.

Here he was, a man who'd played a direct role in the demise of American textiles. I wanted to dislike him, to see him as the enemy. Wasn't he responsible for hurting the people I'd been meeting? But I couldn't. He was just Malik. So our manufacturing decline may have happened to fuel his professional success, but was that his fault? As terrorist attacks and drone strikes in Pakistan put their lives in danger, he'd pulled strings at Indus and moved Raana and their son to Las Vegas. Now, they had found their way to this fledgling dyehouse in Biddeford, Maine.

Still grappling with culture and climate shock, Malik and Raana had thrown themselves headfirst into their work and into helping their son—now a senior in high school—apply to colleges. "God chooses our path, not us," Raana told me with a smile and gentle bob of the head. "So we will be here as long as he wants us to be here."

They were ready to begin working on my yarn. First, they needed to know what color I wanted them to dye it. I learned another interesting and/or disheartening fact: While some people bring fabric snippets or vintage handknits or photos of artwork or landscapes or whatnot, all with the intent of choosing a completely original yarn color, others opt for a much easier path. They bring a sample of a yarn in a color they like. Malik and Raana analyze it under a special light and presto. They have a dye formula.

"So this means I could pull a Quince yarn off the shelves and you'd copy the color for me?" I asked. They both smiled nervously and tilted their heads in a way that said, "Please don't go there."

I'd heard that they preferred to work from Pantone color numbers. Since knitters are always just a step behind the Paris runways (okay, maybe two steps), I pulled up the coming year's Pantone color forecast and rather foolishly chose Pantone 18–3224, otherwise known as Radiant Orchid. A magenta some might describe as "bold." Magenta was the first synthetic color ever created. How fitting that it should be the color for my first big synthetic dye job.

Raana did the first round of heavy lifting, translating my request into just the right small-batch dye formula for a sample. She tinkered with beakers and burners in a small lab until she had two close matches to my color. The three of us stood side by side at a little table with their special full-spectrum lamp shining on the yarn snippets and my original Pantone color chip.

Magenta was the first synthetic color ever created. How fitting that it should be the color for my first big synthetic dye job.

Malik picked one that didn't quite match. Raana disagreed in the most masterfully indirect way. She paused and made "mmmm" sounds as he talked, deftly leading him to choose what she'd wanted all along, a shade somewhere between the two, and to think it was his idea. Satisfied, she scaled her recipe to suit 120 pounds of fiber that we'd dye in the four-hundred-pound tank, the biggest in the dyehouse.

In addition to Raana there was a young man named David, who had quickly learned the ropes from Don. A diesel mechanic by training, he eventually grew tired of working outdoors in Maine winters at a job that was brutal on his body. When his wife got pregnant he knew it was time to stop. "They couldn't pay me enough," he said.

David's day involves a near-constant shuffling of materials from bin to tank to extractor and back onto poles, or "sticks" as they call them—when not fixing broken motors, that is.

"You've got great new equipment being made in England, Australia, Pakistan, and China," he said, "but there's no money to bring it here. Textiles have died so much in the U.S., all we've got is the old stuff."

My yarn had already been moved off the S&D cones and wound into skeins. They were heaped in a big bin with a label that said "Clara Parks." (If I had a dime for every time the "e" was left out of my last name I'd have enough money to start a dyehouse of my own.) One by one, each skein would need to be slipped onto one of the metal poles that fit inside the dye tank.

We had two jobs going that day. First, we would load the biggest tank with the 120 pounds to dye. Second, we would put the remaining sixty pounds of yarn into a smaller tank for scouring. I wanted people to have one skein of each so they could see the yarn before and after it had been dyed.

By the time I arrived, David had finished loading up the large tank and was getting ready to load the smaller one.

I asked him how he knew how many skeins to put on each pole. He smiled and pulled out a calculator and began explaining. "You see, you take 120 and divide by 2.2062, which gets you pounds to kilograms, to grams, approximately sixty times one thousand kilograms, divided by one hundred, which gives you . . ." I regretted asking. All I know is that the final number was twenty-seven skeins per pole.

"Are you naturally good at math?" I asked.

"I'm pretty much good at everything I've tried," he said. "But you've got to care."

I remembered David at S&D referring to one of his clients having "a lotta moxie," and I thought the expression fit this David rather perfectly, too.

Meanwhile, he was busy telling me how the yarn to be scoured would spend ten minutes in the tank with a detergent he described as "eco-friendly." There's no agitation, just the movement of water as it's gently pushed in one direction, then the other.

When the ten minutes were up, the yarn tank would be lifted out of the water, placed on a metal cart, and moved to an extractor that spins at 2,200 RPMs.

"You've gotta make sure it's really balanced," he said, sliding armloads of wet skeins off the poles and dropping them into what appeared to be a very old industrial laundry machine. "If you don't, the whole thing'll just take off."

He tucked a piece of cloth over the top opening, closed the lid, and pushed a big button. As soon as it started spinning, David pointed to an opening in the PVC pipe leading away from the machine. I could see water gurgling through it.

Drier but certainly not dry, the scoured skeins were pulled out of the extractor, dropped into a big bin, and wheeled over to the main area of the dyehouse, where each skein was slipped onto a worn wooden pole and hung on big metal racks to dry.

Scouring was quick, but dyeing would require more time.

We were now standing at the big four-hundred-pound tank which, this being Halloween, took on the sinister look of a giant steel coffin. I didn't see what caused it, but suddenly a thick foam appeared on the surface. I caught someone pouring a white powder into the tanks and was told it was an organic defoamer.

Sure enough, the water soon ran clear again. Next came acetic acid, a much more concentrated version of the vinegar hand-dyers use to assist with dye uptake. (Acetic acid is 56 percent acidity to vinegar's 0.5 percent, meaning they don't have to use nearly as much to get the job done.)

The dye tank runs in two cycles: The water is pushed from one side to the other along the top, and after four minutes it stops and reverses direction, but this time with the water flowing along the bottom of the tank. The goal is to keep dye in constant circulation to prevent spotting or pooling.

Wet yarn can be quite heavy, so the yarn tanks are mechanically lifted using a giant, rather ominous-looking hook that leads up to metal tracks running along the ceiling.

Standing nearby and holding a cartoonishly large yellow control box also connected by a wire to a motor on the ceiling, Malik moved the yarn-filled box over to the dye-filled tank and slowly lowered it until it was fully submerged.

It's surprising that Stephen King hasn't written a story about this yet, with some unfortunate victim trapped inside that box as it slowly descends into the hot water of doom. I couldn't help it—there was a spooky vibe in the dyehouse that day. Anyone who's grown up in Biddeford will tell you that the mill complex, all four million square feet of it, is haunted. In fact, the town's annual Halloween mill tour sells out months in advance. Apparently it's terrifying. They take you deep into the passages that run beneath the buildings—ones that had at one time been flooded with river water leading to the massive turbines. They let your imagination do the rest.

David grew up around here. I asked him if he thought the place was haunted. He smiled and said, "I'm not dumb enough to say it ain't."

Malik had tied several short strands of my yarn to the handle of a little door on top of the tank. This allowed him to cut off one strand every once in a while, pull its dyed tail out of the tank, rinse it and dry it, and check its progress against our original color.

At first the yarn was too pink. More blue was weighed, dissolved in hot water, and added to the mix. Already I could see that the electric fuchsia was way too intense for Eugene's gentle fibers, but it was too late. He would definitely stand back, tilt his head, and declare it garish.

The box was raised out of the dye tank so that Malik could open the door, shove a metal pole inside, and push the skeins apart while shining a light on the yarn to check for saturation. He did this a few times before I declared it "perfect," only out of fear that any further tinkering would make the finished results glow in the dark.

It was nearing 5 p.m. We'd finished the dyeing, and David, Malik, and Raana had left for the day. A skeleton crew remained to help load the extractor with my wet, now definitely garish yarn. Outside, the light was already dimming. I imagined that trick-or-treaters were beginning to assemble. We put one more batch of yarn through the extractor, rolled it into the other room, and hung each skein on the poles. The dyehouse was now eerily quiet.

They'd turned off all the lights in the room with the steel dye tank of doom, giving it an even more forbidding air of a crypt. Now the only sound was that of a small fan blowing air around the drying racks.

I turned to one of the men who'd pitched in to help with this last bit, a true Biddefordian whose family had worked at the mill for generations. I asked him if he thought the place was haunted.

"Have you seen those tunnels that run underneath here?" he asked.

I shook my head.

"They go for miles and miles."

He narrowed his eyes and, in his best ghost-story voice, said, "Go down there and you'll feel it. You know bad stuff has gone on down there. You know people have died."

Then he shrugged, smiled, and wished me good night.

Just like that, my bale was done. I still had to twist and label every skein (I'd been writing all my bale yarn labels by hand; it felt only fitting) and send them to subscribers. And I still needed to share this final step in the journey with them before bringing our schooling to a close. But I'd reached the end of my bale.

There was no graduation ceremony that December, just a few final words of closure and thanks to these patient and trusting people who had made the journey with me. A virtual commencement speech of sorts. I struggled to leave them on an upbeat note, but I kept coming back to the words "if only."

"If only Bollman's still operated its scouring facility in Pennsylvania," I wrote to them. "If only someone still made parts for the old carding machines, spinning frames, twisters, and skeiners domestic producers rely on to make yarn. If only companies like L.L.Bean hadn't moved all their garment production overseas. If only we still had a thriving textiles industry in this country. If only the Great White Bale could go on forever."

But of course it couldn't. I was done.

Into each final yarn package, I tucked a small blue and gold enamel pin I'd had made just for us. It was shaped like the kind of rosette ribbon you'd win at the state fair—only here, it had the figure of a sheep standing on a bale. Under it were the words "Goodwool Ambassador."

There may be no such thing as a Master's of Yarn-Making degree, at least not yet. But we can still use this newly acquired knowledge to make a difference. All we have to do is wear wool and talk about wool and help people understand just how much goes into it—and why it deserves our support.

The world is waiting. Now it's your turn. Go forth, my friend. Be a goodwool ambassador.

CHAPTER 13

CASTING OFF

WHAT DOES ONE DO WITH a newly minted Master's of Yarn-Making degree? What kind of career path opens wide to you after adding an MYM to your résumé? That became the next question. Armed with this new knowledge, would I return to reviewing yarn but with greater flourish and wisdom? Or would I set out on a new adventure?

I'd jumped in headfirst and heart open, trusting in the process to take me where I'd need to be for whatever was next. The problem was, I got to the end of my bale, I'd spun my four chosen yarns, sent them off to the Explorers, and marked the project complete, but "next" wasn't at all clear. Everyone was asking what my next project would be and if they could sign up right then. They were lovely, trusting, eager people. But in fact, "next" was blurrier than ever, and I had another two thousand pounds of wool that needed to become yarn.

It took me several years to work through the rest of what I'd greedily amassed like a newly flush wool oligarch. Only then was I able to step backward and view this journey in its entirety.

I had named this project the Great White Bale without ever actually having read *Moby-Dick*—a move that turned out to be perhaps more prophetic than I could have imagined. I'd figured I was Ahab, that kooky ship captain who was obsessed with a great white whale. Sounded right to me.

But in actual fact (I still haven't read the book, but at least now I know more of the plot), Ahab's quest was fueled entirely by vengeance. He'd already faced the whale once and done battle with it, and the whale had bitten off his leg at the knee. Now, Ahab was out for revenge.

There was no vengeance here. I had no vendetta against the bale, only curiosity. I felt an eagerness to get inside something that had been elusive—the inner workings of the American textiles industry, as seen through the tiny window of yarn.

The identity of the whale changed through the course of the journey. At first it was the bale itself, this mythical behemoth that had overturned my complacent life. But there was very little chasing to be done, and soon enough I had the bale under my control. I'd broken its bands and disemboweled it.

Then, this wee bale of wool, sourced from a New York farm that would make the Montana ranches scoff, became my personal whaling ship. I sailed that wool from place to place. At each stop, I met people who, like the crews the *Pequod* encountered on its crazed captain's quest, shared stories of their encounter with an even fiercer whale: change. Globalization. While some hoped for vengeance, the majority were simply glad to still be alive.

Chasing this whale would have been futile. There is no vengeance against change. You can harpoon it until you run out of harpoons, and you'll never bring it down. But you can grieve the wake it has left behind and figure out how best to thrive in these new waters.

By the end of my journey it had all become so familiar—the smell of the lanolin and the spinning oil, the maker's marks on the machines, the stray tufts of fiber on every surface, the greased gears and spare parts tucked here and there, the endless buckets of empty bobbins, the sights and sounds of the cards and the spinning frames and even the occasional "thwoooop" and hiss of the air splicer. I'd become fond of it, and the people behind it.

There is no vengeance against change. You can harpoon it until you run out of harpoons, and you'll never bring it down.

Those who make this world go—at Chargeurs, Bollman, ASI, S&D, Kraemer, Bartlett, Blackberry Ridge, the Saco River Dyehouse, and elsewhere—are the face of a story that's unfolding across the country, a story that's been unfolding for decades, one that will continue to unfold until we can find a way to slow the tide. By perseverance, flexibility, and a fair share of small mercies, this infrastructure remains intact, at least for now. It has kept people gainfully employed when work of this kind is harder and harder to find. It has enabled smaller companies—including those supplying yarn to knitters—to produce consistently good wool products in this country without going broke. And the passionate consumerism of knitters has allowed Jennifer, Kristine, Adrienne, and those like them to make a living from applying color to yarn. Together, it has kept open the possibility for people to clothe themselves with materials sourced from our own soil.

It's been fun to learn how yarn is made, to do something different, to ease my professional ennui. But all that feels quite superficial in the face of these people's lives and livelihoods, which are on the line. I felt remiss that I hadn't taken the human consequences of this project more seriously.

If we want to be able to make wool socks or sweaters or suits or, yes, yarns, domestically and at prices that are even remotely affordable to the average consumer (and if we want jobs that will allow the average consumer to afford these goods), we need this infrastructure to remain healthy. Whether it's shepherding or shearing or scouring or spinning or dyeing, I keep coming back to the fact that each of these links in our chain is in peril. These are not a museum to the past. Each deserves strengthening.

The glory days of American manufacturing may be behind us. We simply don't live in that world anymore. The United States produces less than 1 percent of the world's wool, and wool itself represents barely over 1 percent of the world's textile fibers.

But that doesn't mean we should give up. Ours will be a new textiles world. Like the one David Schmidt carved from his family legacy, it will be smaller, smarter, safer, more regionalized and efficient, and gentler on the environment. I have every faith in this new world. We just need to keep moving toward it.

The motion was there even during the year that I chased my bale around. A couple in Asheville, North Carolina, successfully raised funds to start an entirely U.S.-based business manufacturing custom-fit cotton and wool sweaters. Jake Bronstein's Kickstarter campaign to start a domestically produced shoelace business raised more than $100,000 over its $25,000 goal—and since then he has raised another $1 million for an American-made hoodie allegedly so well made it comes with a ten-year warranty and free mending. NPR's *Planet Money* produced an amazing piece on the production of a common T-shirt. The Saco River Dyehouse surpassed its initial fundraising goals by more than $16,000, and Mendocino Wool and Fiber exceeded its own fundraising goal to start a fiber mill in Northern California.

It continues. Detroit now has a watch factory. You can buy U.S.-made jeans whose fabric, hardware, and leather have all been sourced in this country. Ditto socks. Outdoor clothing retailer Duckworth goes so far as to source all its wool from a single Montana ranch.

The American Woolen Company, which at one time produced 20 percent of all woolen fabric in this country, has been reborn and is manufacturing fine woolen fabric and men's clothing out of the old Warren of Stafford Textile Mill in Connecticut. The company received venture capital from investors who saw not only nostalgia but growth potential in this industry.

Just outside of Sacramento, Ryan Huston and his wife, Kat, have launched a new mill, Huston Textile Co., dedicated to providing small-batch American-made fabrics from U.S.-sourced materials, working with restored textile equipment also made in America.

Along with a growing number of farmers, sheep ranchers are embracing farming practices that sequester so much additional carbon dioxide (both in plants and in sheep's wool) that they can operate with a carbon-neutral footprint and an impressive degree of environmental sustainability.

A growing network of "fibershed" programs that began in California has spread across the country, helping link regional farmers, wool producers, manufacturers, and consumers.

Advances are being made even in the realm of machine-washable wool, as we become increasingly aware of the harm microplastics are doing to the environment. The synthetic polymer used in the chlorine-polymer shrink-resist system is slowly being replaced with biodegradable ecopolymers, and the chlorine with cleaner enzymes.

The wool market may be at a seventy-year low, but it's remained steady for a decade. Globally, the price of fine wools has risen to an all-time high. In the United States, so many major manufacturers have swooped in and snatched up the fine wool clip that smaller businesses are having a hard time sourcing domestic wool for their own products. We need more ranches to enter the game.

Change is happening.

All of this is in response to rising consumer demand and a willingness to pay a premium for domestically made goods. Just like Ladd said, the answer to our wool problem is quite simple: people using it. As the saying goes, supply may win the battle, but demand wins the war.

But we still have the aging problem. Not nearly enough is being done upstream to inspire new people to enter the field, especially young people. Everywhere you look, those who've been doing this their whole lives are now retiring, whether it's small farmers or midsize ranchers or full-scale sheep producers—shearers or scourers or processors or even scientists or small-ruminant specialists. Without the professors and university courses and active programs for school-aged kids, we risk closing off this world from the next generation. At an ASI speech a few years ago, renowned animal behaviorist Dr. Temple Grandin urged the industry to keep these avenues of exposure open. The only way young people will know if they want to be a part of this industry, she kept repeating, is if they are exposed to it.

Back in my world, much has changed in the intervening years since my own exposure to the bale began.

Emboldened by my MYM degree and embarrassed by my ineptitude at Eugene's farm on shearing day, I went back to school and obtained my Level 1 ASI certification in wool classing. Sadly, I will never be able to impress Eugene with my newfound wool-skirting skills. He left us on May 29, 2018, before I had a chance to tell him I was writing this book.

The Wool Trust Fund has been given several more budgetary reprieves, allowing ASI to continue its mission. Its Instagram feed is still limping along.

Ladd still keeps Bollman operations steady. Longer wait times suggest that business continues to boom, despite Woolrich having just closed its iconic mill in Woolrich, Pennsylvania, and moved everything overseas. The rebirth of the American Woolen Co. is helping to fill the hole Woolrich leaves behind.

Back in Maine, Lindsey Rice has bought a four-bowl Sargents Scouring Train of his own and is now offering scouring as part of his fiber-processing services. His wife and daughter attended wool-classing school with me and hinted at even bigger plans for the mill, including Global Organic Textile Standard Certification.

Having finally decided to slow down, Anne and Marc have put Blackberry Ridge up for sale. They have no takers yet. Until then, Anne continues to play beautiful music with her equipment.

Kristine and Adrienne are still flourishing in the Bay Area. Occasionally Adrienne finds walnut-dyed raccoon footprints around a new gelato tub of walnuts that is in its third year of aging on the back patio.

Kraemer carries on with its wholesale yarn and pattern business. Victor's dog, Mocha, has since departed for the great air-conditioned office in the sky. Eleanor has finally retired and is traveling the globe. The mill was tapped to help spin yarn for the 2014 and 2018 Winter Olympic Games uniforms, and hand-dyers continue to top off an order list that keeps the machines humming.

Our Texas road trip turned out to be good practice for Jennifer Heverly, now Jennifer Tepper. Her kids having headed off to college, Jen has decided to leave her tree house behind, along with her husband's deer heads (and her now ex-husband), and start a new life for herself in the wilds of New Mexico. She's curious what colors the Southwest will inspire in her yarn.

In Massachusetts, things have taken a turn. The U.S. Navy announced plans to phase out its iconic wool peacoat from the Seabag Requirements List and replace it with a 100 percent synthetic winter parka. The move has the potential to devastate several New England textiles companies. I haven't the stomach to ask S&D how they'll fare. But I know that they still have one more year on that baseball contract before it comes up for renewal. (Seriously, anyone out there want to start a sweater company with me?)

The Saco River Dyehouse has moved out of Biddeford and across the river to a modern industrial park in Saco. They've changed the name to Maine Dye & Textiles and gone through several new rounds of crowdfunding. Malik and Raana's son is now ensconced in medical school, and they are no longer with the dyehouse. Claudia did away with the old poles and metal racks in favor of a space-age microwave yarn dryer that looks like a drive-through toaster and gets yarn dry in a matter of hours instead of days. They've left the drafty charm of the old mill behind—its romance, its authenticity, its historical significance—in favor of practicality and efficiency. Just before this book went to press, the dyehouse filed for Chapter 11 bankruptcy protection, citing problems with their landlord. But Claudia still remains optimistic.

It can be easy for those of us who know how to knit or sew or crochet or weave our own clothing to feel smug. We have a magic weapon. We still have the capacity to create our own long-lasting garments using materials we can seek out ourselves, ones we can trace all the way back to their source if we want—to the farm, to the field, to the sheep.

We are makers, but it's also important to remember that we are consumers. In each step of our own creative process, through our purchases and our attention, there is an opportunity to reinforce the work of those we believe are moving us forward in a positive direction. It's a collective power that has the potential to become great.

This means being aware of where our yarn and clothing comes from. It also means being more cognizant of the people, communities, cultures, corporations, and traditions that our money is helping to support. These people's products will become an intimate part of our daily lives, bending and stretching and breathing right along with us. Just as we are vigilant about the food that goes into our bodies, so we must be more mindful of what we put on them.

There's a common conception that wool, especially domestic wool, is too expensive for many people. I agree it can be prohibitive. But knitters, a worsted-weight skein of Brown Sheep Nature Spun yarn, made in Nebraska of American wool, at 310 yards (283 m) per skein, will cost about $9. Less if you find it on sale. That puts the bill for a medium-sized women's pullover at about $36. And for roughly the cost of five venti caramel macchiatos, you can get a pair of thick wool socks from Duckworth, which sources all its wool from a single Montana ranch. American wool needn't always be out of reach.

Just as we are vigilant about the food that goes into our bodies, so we must be more mindful of what we put on them.

Meanwhile, Eugene's flock, now under Dominique's care, remains blissfully unaware. They simply keep following her around, lovestruck, hoping for treats and growing wool for her, year after year, without fail.

The more ways we can find to use their coats, the longer these animals get to be with us, the richer the lives will be for all those who work with them and their wool, and, I'd like to think, the better the world we'll get to live in.

I still don't know what I'll do with my Master's of Yarn-Making degree. But I do know I'll never look at a skein of wool yarn the same way again.

ACKNOWLEDGMENTS

While this journey took place entirely in the United States, it is in no way intended to be a nativist manifesto. What has happened to the American wool industry has happened to the wool industry around the world. A noble and worthy fiber that used to dominate our closets now barely exceeds 1 percent of what we wear. In its place, we're being sold fibers that come from an oil barrel and that do not breathe or biodegrade, that readily ignite and melt, and that, in short, do not deserve to be our second skin.

This book honors all those people, around the world, who've chosen to link their own well-being with that of sheep. Wool begins with them. They're the ones who treat sheep for injuries and ailments, who barely get a wink of sleep during lambing season, who remove the sheep's heavy winter coats every spring, who make the terribly hard decision of who stays and who must go for the good of the flock—and who get the tractor and dig a hole every time someone doesn't make it. They are my heroes. It's a hard and unglamorous life, but it has meaning and value, and I, for one, am grateful.

Adventures don't happen in a void. They occur because, at each juncture, someone is there who believes in you and encourages you onward. For me, that vital support staff began with my Knitter's Review Retreat family. Without their faith and encouragement, I'm confident you'd be reading someone else's book right now.

There weren't enough pages here to list every fellow graduate of my Master's of Yarn-Making program by name, but they will forever occupy a very special place in my heart. We had quite a time together. As for those who'd hoped the Great White Bale would be my downfall, I'm sorry I failed to deliver that catastrophic failure. Have faith and stick around. Tomorrow's another day.

Endless gratitude goes to my friend Jane Cochran, who jumped in to wrangle spreadsheets and take care of people in the best possible way. I am indebted to Pam Allen for giving me a place to park my bale, and to Claudia Raessler for so generously offering help at each step of the way. I also must tip my (felted wool) hat both to my agent, Elizabeth Kaplan, for being such a fine lighthouse and gatekeeper, and to my publisher, Shawna Mullen, lover of words and wool in equal measure.

The Blue Hill Public Library was my refuge while I pulled all the final strands of this book together. No greater public institution ever existed than that of the public library. And my beloved Clare kept the home fires burning not once but twice—first while I was living the year, and again while I was writing about it.

That said, this book owes its biggest debt of gratitude to a person who is no longer here. Eugene's absence deserves more explanation than simply "he left us." To me it perfectly, albeit tragically, distills his very essence as a person.

Eugene had been diagnosed with a progressive neurological syndrome that was already beginning to rob him of his language capabilities and would eventually lead to dementia. As it got worse and while he was still able, Eugene did what he'd done for every ailing sheep in his flock: He put himself on the truck. By which I mean he sent Dominique a final text, walked out into his garden, and shot himself. A responsible shepherd, he practiced what he preached until the very end.

Countless times since then I've wished I could consult with him about this story. Or just let him know that the book was in the works. Instead, I relied on notes and emails and photographs and Dominique, who willingly revisited that room of grief over and over again so that I could get the facts right.

Oh, but Eugene did keep me company. Hudson Valley photographer Francesco Mastalia had captured Eugene for his "Portraits of New Yorkers" series. After Eugene died, our mutual friend Robin Ringo sent me a framed print of Mastalia's portrait. It hung on the wall right behind my desk so that that Eugene could oversee the completion of this book. I asked for his help; I complained; I may have even begged once or twice. He urged me ever forward, and we toasted when I hit "send" on the final manuscript.

If I look closely, he's smiling right now.

INDEX